* Edward S
p 284

The Vi...
Civility

David Adams
Lima Ohio
June 2024

* p. 108 "little magazines" for which Epstein wrote
* p. 33 small notepad in shirt pocket for "my stuff"
* p. 208 Epstein is a writer
* p. 210 WS Journal
* p. 225 unwanted words
* p. 213 "American Scholar" editor
* p. 228 fired as editor
* p. 234 Saul Bellow
* p. 236 Max Weber (also p. 104)
** p. 236 Edward Shils on religion (p. 238) "a pious agnostic*"
* pp. 244-245 poem about Shils
* p. 252 Wall street Journal
* p. 257 being 86

*f*P

ALSO BY JOSEPH EPSTEIN

Divorced in America: Marriage in an Age of Possibility (1974)

Familiar Territory: Observations on American Life (1979)

Ambition: The Secret Passion (1980)

The Middle of My Tether: Familiar Essays (1983)

Plausible Prejudices: Essays on American Writing (1985)

Once More Around the Block: Familiar Essays (1987)

Partial Payments: Essays on Writers and Their Lives (1989)

The Goldin Boys: Stories (1991)

A Line Out for a Walk: Familiar Essays (1991)

Pertinent Players: Essays on the Literary Life (1993)

With My Trousers Rolled: Familiar Essays (1995)

Life Sentences: Literary Essays (1997)

Narcissus Leaves the Pool: Familiar Essays (1999)

Snobbery: The American Version (2002)

Envy (2003)

Fabulous Small Jews: Stories (2003)

Alexis de Tocqueville: Democracy's Guide (2006)

Friendship: An Exposé (2006)

In a Cardboard Belt!: Essays Personal, Literary, and Savage (2007)

Fred Astaire (2008)

The Love Song of A. Jerome Minkoff and Other Stories (2010)

Gossip: The Untrivial Pursuit (2011)

Essays in Biography (2012)

Distant Intimacy: A Friendship in the Age of the Internet (2013)
(with Frederic Raphael)

A Literary Education and Other Essays (2014)

Masters of the Games: Essays and Stories on Sport (2015)

Frozen in Time: Twenty Stories (2016)

Wind Sprints: Shorter Essays (2016)

Where Were We?: The Conversation Continues (2017)
(with Frederic Raphael)

Charm: The Elusive Enchantment (2018)

The Ideal of Culture: Essays (2018)

Gallimaufry: A Collection of Essays, Reviews, Bits (2020)

The Novel, Who Needs It? (2023)

Never Say You've Had a Lucky Life

Especially If You've Had a Lucky Life

Joseph Epstein

FREE PRESS
New York London Toronto Sydney New Delhi

Free Press
An Imprint of Simon & Schuster, LLC
1230 Avenue of the Americas
New York, NY 10020

First Frees Press hardcover edition April 2024

FREE PRESS and colophon are registered trademarks of Simon & Schuster, LLC

Simon & Schuster: Celebrating 100 Years of Publishing in 2024

For information about special discounts for bulk purchases, please contact Simon & Schuster Special Sales at 1-866-506-1949 or business@simonandschuster.com.

The Simon & Schuster Speakers Bureau can bring authors to your live event. For more information or to book an event, contact the Simon & Schuster Speakers Bureau at 1-866-248-3049 or visit our website at www.simonspeakers.com.

Interior design by Wendy Blum

Manufactured in the United States of America

10 9 8 7 6 5 4 3 2 1

Library of Congress Cataloging-in-Publication Data

Names: Epstein, Joseph, 1937- author.
Title: Never say you've had a lucky life : especially if you've had a lucky life / by Joseph Epstein.
Description: First Simon & Schuster hardcover edition. | New York : Simon & Schuster, 2024. |
Identifiers: LCCN 2023033963 (print) | LCCN 2023033964 (ebook) | ISBN 9781668009635 (hardcover) | ISBN 9781668009642 (paperback) | ISBN 9781668009673 (ebook)
Subjects: LCSH: Epstein, Joseph, 1937- | Authors, American—20th Century—Biography.
Classification: LCC PS3555.P6527 Z46 2024 (print) | LCC PS3555.P6527 (ebook) | DDC 814/.54—dc23/eng/20231218
LC record available at https://lccn.loc.gov/2023033963
LC ebook record available at https://lccn.loc.gov/2023033964

ISBN 978-1-6680-0963-5
ISBN 978-1-6680-0967-3 (ebook)

To David Zimberoff (1937–2022)

"For fortune is indeed a great weight in the scales; I might almost say it is everything in human affairs."

—Demosthenes

"I could inform the dullest author how he might write an interesting book. Let him relate the events of his own life with honesty, not disguising the feelings that accompanied them."

—Samuel Taylor Coleridge

Contents

Never Say You've Had a Lucky Life

Especially If You've Had a Lucky Life

Introduction

An acquaintance, a man not known for his wide reading, not long ago asked me if I were still writing. I replied that I was and had only recently begun work on an autobiography. "Interesting," he said. "Whose?" The question, I have come to think, is not as dopey as it first sounds, implying as it does that I may not have had a sufficiently interesting life to merit an autobiography.

In a brief essay on the subject of autobiography, Gilbert Highet sets out three main kinds of autobiography: one describing What I Did, another What I Saw, and a third devoted to What I Felt or Endured. The autobiography now in your hands largely eludes all three categories. Over what is now a long life, I did little, saw nothing notably historic, and endured not much out of the ordinary of anguish or trouble or exaltation. What, then, is the justification of this book?

For autobiography requires a justification. The great autobiographies—those by Benvenuto Cellini, Jean-Jacques Rousseau,

Benjamin Franklin, John Stuart Mill, Henry Adams—had as their justification their authors living in historically interesting times, or harboring radically new ideas, or participating in great events, or having famously impressive family connections. My autobiography qualifies on none of these counts. Mine has been a quiet life, unspectacular, fortunate in many ways, but far from dramatic. Why do I feel the need to write my autobiography; quite as important, why do I feel anyone else might be interested in reading it? What is my justification? Two quick, at this point perhaps superficial, answers are: one, because I think my life is in some way emblematic of the times in which I have lived; and two, because I believe that over the years I have acquired the literary skill to recount that life well.

Janet Malcolm, a superior journalist, wrote a brief essay with the title "Thoughts on Autobiography from an Abandoned Autobiography." In it she writes that:

> I have been aware, as I write this autobiography, of a feeling of boredom with the project. My efforts to make what I write interesting seem pitiful. My hands are tied, I feel. I cannot write about myself as I write about the people I have written about as a journalist. To these people I have been a kind of amanuensis: they have dictated their stories to me and I have retold them. They have posed for me and I have drawn their portraits. No one is dictating to me or posing for me now.
>
> Memory is not a journalist's tool. Memory glimmers and hints, but shows nothing sharply or clearly. Memory does not narrate or render character. Memory has no regard for the reader. If an autobiography is to be even minimally readable,

the autobiographer must step in and subdue what you could call memory's autism, its passion for the tedious. He must not be afraid to invent. Above all he must invent himself.

Contra Ms. Malcolm, I side with Ford Madox Ford, who wrote that "genius is memory."

George Orwell wrote of autobiography that it "is only to be trusted when it reveals something disgraceful. A man who gives a good account of himself is probably lying, since any life when viewed from the inside is simply a series of defeats." Alas, in the pages that follow I touch on a disgrace or two, and recount a few defeats, but disgrace and defeat are far from dominating themes in my autobiography. Nor do I have any dark secrets to confess: a hidden pedophilic streak, having stolen money from every job I've ever held, a yearning to transgender myself, a longing to be spanked by an NFL linebacker in a nun's habit.

Rather the reverse: in this book I more often recount my own extraordinary good luck, in the time in which I was born, in the parents to whom I was born, in my education, and much more. In doing so I hope I do not at any point lapse into braggadocio. But the dice of personal destiny thus far do seem to have rolled well for me. The moral I have drawn from the story is expressed in my title, *Never Say You've Had a Lucky Life,* with its subtitle, *Especially If You've Had a Lucky Life.*

In this autobiography I chronicle the culture in which I grew up—petit bourgeois, Jewish, Midwest American—its strengths and weaknesses, the solace it afforded, the blinkers it set in place to narrow my outlook, and finally my changing relation to that culture. The city of Chicago plays a background role in the book, for I have lived all but seven years of my life there. Chicago, which has a well-established place in our national literary history, has bred many writers, perhaps owing to the attractions of its quotidian life and its low but steady view of human nature.

I have long considered myself to have drawn a lucky ticket in the parent lottery, and I provide here portraits of my parents and set out their views on child-rearing, so different than those reigning in our day. But not of their views on child-rearing only. My parents and those of their generation existed in what I have come to believe a pre-therapeutic state. If I had told my father—a kind and in every way honorable man—that I felt "insecure" about a new job or relationship, I am fairly certain he would not have understood what I was talking about and abjured me to knock off this "insecurity talk" and "be a man."

I know little about my mother's father, about whom she rarely spoke, and only toward the end of her own life did I learn that he had committed suicide. (Probably, I have since assumed, from depression.) Not only did my mother never wish to talk about this but, more extraordinarily, she also kept this information from her husband, a man with whom she lived in a loving and happy marriage for fifty-seven years. (My father learned about it from one of his sisters-in-law. "But your mother doesn't know I know," he told me.) I don't believe my mother, a strong and highly intelligent woman, suffered from failing to talk about her father's sad end; she merely saw no need to talk about it. For her, then in her adolescence, it must have been a devastating event when it occurred, possibly a shameful one, but talking about it would change nothing, so why bother? Such was life in a non-therapeutic age, so radically different from our own.

The chief portion of this book is devoted to my own development,  psychological, intellectual, literary. Born in 1937, mine was a happy boyhood, lived on playgrounds, where I was a slightly better-than-average athlete; hanging around drug- and school stores, where I was a wise-guy-wit; at high school dances, where I was a rhumba king; and at drive-in movies, where I was never allowed to go as far with the young girls of my generation as I ardently desired. I never set out to be the writer, editor, university teacher, intellectual I eventually became. I was an entirely uninterested student through grammar and high school—and not all that spectacular when I eventually ended up an undergraduate at the University of Chicago. Had you asked me when I was seventeen what I intended to do with my later life I should probably have answered that, like my father, I might be a salesman, and, with luck and a certain amount of diligence, eventually own my own business. ("Only a schmuck works for someone else" is perhaps the first precept from the book of Chicago Jewish wisdom.) I don't believe I had heard the word "intellectual" before I was nineteen. In any case, the type of the intellectual wouldn't have much impressed me had I encountered any of the species. As for "a man of letters," I would have assumed he was someone who worked in a post office.

Pages here are devoted to my two years as a drafted enlisted man in the peacetime U.S. Army (1958–1960), with some comment on the advantages of the draft, at least for young men. I was never enchanted by or especially proud of being in the army, which is one of those experiences that look better the further one is from it. But without the interference of the draft I might have gone off to law school and a life perhaps more prosperous but distinctly less satisfying than the one I have been allowed to lead.

Domestic details are taken up in these pages. I shan't elaborate here, except to say that having at the age of twenty-three married a woman with two children and having with her two further children, I found myself at the age of twenty-six living in New York on a low salary (as a subeditor of a political magazine), ablaze with ambition and fettered by frustration, and with nothing but darkish prospects in sight.

Portions of this book are devoted to my days in Little Rock, Arkansas, where I was the director of the county's anti-poverty program during the heightened years of the civil rights movement. Others to my years as a senior editor at *Encylopaedia Britannica*, where I worked with Mortimer Adler and Robert Hutchins on a project to reconstruct, but eventually to diminish, what was then the world's greatest reference work. My tenure as the editor of the *American Scholar* is gone into in some detail. How my writing career blossomed will be taken up, and with it the cast of impressive figures who aided me along the way: Saul Bellow, Edward Shils, Hilton Kramer, Irving Howe, and others. My days as a university teacher are recounted, highlighted by the vast changes in the nature of the university from my student through my teaching years.

The underlying theme of my autobiography is living through radical change: from a traditionally moral culture to a therapeutic one, from an era when the extended family was strong to its current diminished status (I have grand-nieces and -nephews I have never met and am unlikely ever to meet), from print to digital life featuring the war of pixel versus print, and much more.

I hope this autobiography, like a good novel, will remind its readers how unpredictable, various, and wondrously rich life, even an outwardly quiet life, can be. As for its justification, I can finally offer none but that which I heard more than sixty years ago, when I attended a lecture given by Stephen Potter, the author of *Lifemanship* and *The Theory and Practice of Gamesmanship*. At that lecture, during the question-and-answer session, a young man got up to ask why Potter, who was also a Coleridge scholar, wrote *Lifesmanship* and other such works in the same comic mode. Potter cleared his throat in a longish English harrumph, then announced, "Out of work, you know."

Chapter One

An Unroyal Mountie

When I open my computer, on my desktop there appears the photograph of a boy—he cannot be much more than three years old—in a Royal Canadian Mounted Police uniform. The uniform, jodhpurs and a jacket with epaulets, has a large badge over the right-hand pocket; from one of the jacket buttons depends a chain with a whistle at its end stuck into a Sam Browne belt. The shoulder strap of the belt is sliding slightly off the boy's left shoulder. The boy has his right hand on a cap pistol in a holster also attached to the belt. The boy is a touch pudgy, his light brown hair is neatly parted on the left, and he has the smile of someone delighted to be in the world. The boy is, of course, me, the photograph appears on the dust jacket of this book, and the book itself is about what happened to him over the more than eight decades of his life.

The reason I wear a Royal Mounted Police uniform instead of a cowboy or a pirate uniform is that my father was a Canadian, who came to the United States, specifically to Chicago, at the age of seventeen to make his fortune, which he did. Some years ago I began the last paragraph of a book I wrote on the subject of ambition with the following words: "We do not choose to be born. We do not choose our parents. We do not choose our historical epoch, or the country of our birth, or the immediate circumstances of our upbringing. . . ." I hope it doesn't make me seem slaphappy when I say I feel extremely lucky in all these realms in which I had no real choice: parents, epoch, country, and throw in religion, city, and social class. This is a book, again, about a man who, though he has known disappointments, setbacks, and a major sadness or two, nonetheless feels himself to have been extraordinarily lucky in life.

I write that last sentence with some hesitation, if not trepidation. In a famous anecdote, Croesus, the vastly wealthy king of Lydia, asks the Athenian sage Solon who the happiest man in the world is, believing himself to be that man. Solon puts forth the name of Tellus of Athens, who has raised excellent sons and now has grandchildren. He then cites two other men who have also achieved modest success, but genuine happiness. He warns Croesus that no one can be certain of his good fortune until his life is over. Croesus, it turns out, will lose his wealth, be captured by the Persian Cyrus, and in one version of the story is said to have thrown himself on a burning pyre, exclaiming, "Solon, thou seer! Oh, Solon, Solon!" thus nicely illustrating that one tempts the furies in thinking one has had a fortunate life before that life is complete. In another version, the Persians kill Croesus by pouring molten gold down his throat.

Yet, risking hubris, I cannot help but think what good luck I have thus far had in my own life. To bring up only a few modest items,

I was able to teach at a university without having to undergo the tedium of acquiring any advanced degrees. I was appointed editor of a magazine, the *American Scholar*, the quarterly journal of Phi Beta Kappa, without having to be concerned about its finances or having been a Phi Beta Kappa myself. I have not had to go into an office over the past fifty or so years. Above all, through my adult life I have been allowed to do the work I love, writing about what I pleased, expressing my true views, and being well rewarded, financially as well as psychologically, while doing so.

I feel not least lucky in the year 1937, in which I was born. The Depression was tailing off, but still cast a dark shadow over American life. One result was that married couples were in some cases choosing not to have children, in others delaying or having fewer children. My own parents waited until my mother was twenty-seven, my father thirty before bringing me into the world. Because of the nervousness about the future brought on by the Depression, mine was a generation with a notably low demographic cohort. So low, I discovered in later years, that, far from the mad fever to get into colleges and universities that bedeviled later and now current generations, colleges and universities of my day actually sought us. The University of Illinois, where I spent the first of my college years, had, in effect, open enrollment; if you lived in the state, you were automatically accepted at the university, even if you finished last in your high school class and had five felonies (accepted, to be sure, on probation, but accepted nevertheless).

To have been born in the late 1930s or early 1940s also meant that you were born at a time when children were not yet at the absolute center of their parents' lives as, for better *and* worse, they subsequently came to be. One was allowed to grow up with greater freedom, fewer constraints, less pressure all round. As for the kind of pressure I mean, today one reads about children from upper-middle-class families who, failing to get into the Ivy League schools of their choice, commit suicide. They do so, I imagine, not only because they are sorely disappointed but also because they feel they feel they have let down the parents who had put in so much effort on their upbringing and whose hope was riding on them.

Ours was the last generation to grow up wishing to become adults as soon as possible. Unlike those who came after us, we had no longing to remain young forever. We came of age before the advent of rock and roll, music that posits the assumption of permanent youthfulness. Instead we listened to Ella Fitzgerald and Frank Sinatra, Julie London and Nat King Cole, Jo Stafford and Dick Haymes, who sang about unrequited love, finding a true love, and other grown-up matters. Philip Larkin, born in 1922 and hence roughly a decade or so older than the members of our generation, nonetheless put our case with his usual comic precision when he claimed to have given up on Christianity, so long as it promised a return to childhood in the afterlife. Larkin, like those of my generation, wanted to be finished with childhood as soon as possible, and to get on with adulthood with its promise of independence and freedom, not to mention, as he did not fail to mention, "liquor, long-play records, beautiful women, keys."

Our parents also had a certain decorum missing from parents of later generations. I do not recall seeing my mother not wearing a dress (or at home what was called a "housecoat") or without makeup. Until his retirement at seventy-five, my father had no leisure clothes. Today, on the streets of my own middle-class neighborhood, I see older men and women go about in flip-flops, cargo shorts, and tank tops, getups my parents wouldn't have worn to take out the garbage.

Nor did mothers of my parents' generation, at least not the middle-class ones among them, breastfeed their children. Breastfeeding tends to go in and out of fashion, and in the 1930s, '40s, and early '50s, it was distinctly out of fashion, and thought peasanty. Some psychiatrists—Karen Horney among them—put great emphasis on the importance of breastfeeding, and doubtless many among them would find those of us who went without it greatly deprived and might attribute unpleasant or sad qualities to us owing to this deprivation. We, however, never noticed, nor felt any sense of deprivation.

The parents of our generation were nowhere near so child-centered as subsequent generations of parents. Their own lives often came before those of their children. Numerous examples of this can be adduced, but a notable one I have observed is that in so many families among my contemporaries there is a five- or six-year hiatus between the birth of the first- and second-born child (my own brother is five and a half years younger than I). Parents, my sense is, decided to have a second child only after the first was enrolled in school; in other words, they considered their own convenience first. A five-year separation in age, meanwhile, provides an almost certain discouragement of closeness between siblings, at least while growing up, but, then, one can't win in every way.

To return to the eager rush to adulthood of my generation, it was not without its pitfalls. A serious one among them may well have been too-early marriage. We tended to marry in our early twenties. A woman not yet married by twenty-five was thought in danger of a life of spinsterhood. I have never seen statistics on the subject, but my guess is that the divorce rate has been high among us, and our real marriages, like my own, have been our second marriages.

As for sex, not a lot of it was available to us. We came of age B.P., or Before the Pill, which made sex a highly risky business—risky chiefly for girls and young women, who were vulnerable on two grounds: pregnancy and loss of reputation. Sex outside marriage was for them a danger, and may indeed have contributed to the propensity of our generation for early marriage. The danger, and the rarity, of sex may also have had a deleterious effect on a generation of novelists—from Norman Mailer through Philip Roth—causing them to overemphasize the drama and excitement of sex in their fiction.

Ours has been called—stigmatized as, really—"the silent generation." The label, meant to denote our lack of enthusiasm for political action, was first affixed during the middle and late 1960s, when the student and anti–Vietnam War protests got underway in boisterous earnest. Most of the males among those of my generation had already served in the peacetime army, when the draft was still in non-disputable effect. (I recall a photograph of the singer Joan Baez and two other young women appearing under a Vietnam War protest poster bearing the caption "Girls Say Yes to Boys Who Say No.") The sixties were really a single-persons affair. Many of us from my generation by then had families, which meant that the culture of the sixties—drugs, easy sex, no rush about finding work—wasn't for us. I had two stepsons, both in their teens, and I recall listening to their talk of drugs with more worry than interest, and indeed a few of their friends died from overdoses.

Besides, the anti-Americanism implicit in the sixties protest movement wasn't readily available to us who grew up in the midst of America's last "good war." As kids we watched war movies, from which we came away proud to be American. Most of us had relatives or neighbors who had gone off to fight in that war. We did not, we could not, look upon the United States as a racist, cruelly capitalist, essentially corrupt country in need of revolutionary change. We thought, most of us still think, the United States, for all its flaws, the most interesting, the most generous, the grandest country in the world.

Our generation also came of age before what has been called "the therapeutic culture" kicked in. The doctrines of Sigmund Freud, Carl Jung, Wilhelm Reich, and others had more than a foot in the door before our birth, but they did not permeate the culture in the way they would come to do, and still do, even though the doctrines of most of them no longer hold sway. Our parents' culture and that which came long before them was about the formation of character; the therapeutic culture was about achieving happiness. The former was about courage and honor, the latter about self-esteem and freedom from stress.

Our parents were, for the most part, pre-psychological in their outlook. If I had told my father that I sorely felt the sting of an unresolved Oedipus complex, he would have had to ask what that was and after learning about it would have laughed at the absurdity of it.

My mother, a highly intelligent and immensely secure woman, spent the last few years of her life with liver cancer and, though she underwent the torture of chemotherapy, was fairly certain she would not survive it. I one day mentioned to a friend my mother's probably terminal cancer, and he replied by telling me that there are many excellent support groups for people with terminal illnesses.

I could easily imagine my mother's response to my suggestion that she join such a group. "Let me understand your suggestion," she might say. "You feel that if I sit in a room with strangers and listen to their problems and then tell them my own, I shall emerge feeling better. Is this what you're suggesting? Is this the kind of idiot I raised as a son?"

The therapeutic culture, surely, is behind the way children are currently brought up, which is to say as eminently fragile creatures. The triumph of the therapeutic—the phrase supplies the title of Philip Rieff's important book on the subject—has altered the ideal of manhood and womanhood. Without the imposition of the therapeutic, political correctness, presumably meant to preserve the self-esteem of women and minorities but often used to destroy the lives of people thought political enemies, would never have gained the hold in contemporary life that it now has.

Finally, there has been the advent of the computer and with it the digital revolution. With its social media, its changing the way people shop, take in news, express opinions, attack and praise one another, the digital revolution may ultimately be more decisive than the invention of the printing press and, four centuries later, the motorcar.

Plus ça change, plus c'est la même chose, the more things change, the more they stay the same. This most popular of aphorisms, though it has some application to human nature, does not otherwise have a very high truth content, at least not to me when I think of the radical changes that have occurred in my lifetime: from fountain pens to smartphones, from cumbersome condoms to birth control pills, from intolerance of homosexuality to exultant acceptance of sexual reassignment surgery, from the high value placed on selfless sacrifice to that now placed on self-regard in so many realms of life. The notion of change that distinctly does not stay the same plays throughout this book, if not quite providing its theme. *Plus ça change*, if I may be permitted to edit the aphorism, *plus ça change.*

Chapter Two

A Winning Ticket in the Parents Lottery

In the parents lottery, I drew a winning ticket, having a father and mother I respected, admired, loved. Neither had much in the way of formal education. My father never finished high school; my mother took what was called "the commercial course"—typing, dictation, bookkeeping, and other secretarial skills—at John Marshall High School on the then largely Jewish West Side of Chicago. I never saw my mother read a book, including any of those I have written. If either wanted me to become a "professional man"—that is, physician, dentist, lawyer, CPA—they never mentioned it. In fact, neither ever spoke about my future. One of their gifts to me was to allow me to go at things my own way, unencumbered by their desires.

My mother was the third born of five children, and a very strange quintet they were. Her older sister, Ceil, who married a man who worked in delicatessens, I never saw smile. One of her two younger sisters, Sally, married a cabdriver, whom she later divorced, and presented herself as working-class, saying "youse" and "dems" and other such locutions, and was comfortable in her neighborhood bar. Florence, her youngest sister, whom I much loved when I was a child, lived out most of her life in a shroud of depression, at one point having to enter a mental institution, leaving her son for roughly five years in the care of my parents.

My mother's one brother, Samuel, second born among her siblings, was a gambler, eventually a bookmaker, who lived most of his life in Los Angeles. He owned a few points in the Riviera Hotel and Casino in Vegas, and had not one but two nicknames: "Lefty" and "Square Sam." I scarcely knew him, but recall being in his company on one occasion when, for the better part of the time, he held a radio to his ear, listening, doubtless, to incoming sports scores. I recall him wearing a novel (to me) three-piece suit: trousers, jacket, and matching topcoat. Sinatra is said to have attended his granddaughter's wedding. His one child, a son, Alan, owned a bar and grill in Los Angeles called Sneaky Pete's, patronized by Johnny Carson and other show business glitterati. Alan died in his forties of alcoholism. My mother attended her brother Sam's funeral. She returned to report that he had twenty-seven ultra-suede jackets in his closet, and that the funeral was ravaged by the appearance at it of her dead brother's mistress.

My mother had a great love for her mother, the matriarch and head of the family. She, my grandmother, came to America from England, from the city of Leeds, no doubt by way of somewhere in Eastern Europe. She was alive when I was born, but died before I could acquire any strong memories of her. She had an English maid, a woman named Minnie Tumbletee, whose husband, Ted, a retired sergeant in the British army, spoke with an indecipherable working-class

English accent. I once asked my mother how her mother, who was far from wealthy, could afford a full-time maid. She told me that the money, $100 a month, came from my mother's sister in Leeds, who had caught her husband, a well-to-do cap manufacturer, with a lover, and as part of the penalty for his getting caught and for her staying with him, he had to mail $100 monthly to her sister in Chicago. My grandmother spent the money on Minnie's salary. Minnie used to send me an annual birthday card with a dollar bill in it until I was thirty. Perhaps she felt that at thirty I could manage without her financial support.

Belle was my mother's name; *belle*, "beautiful" in French. She was not herself beautiful but handsome, attractive, stunning even. A friend of my wife described my mother as looking like a Spanish princess. She dressed elegantly, and went off to the beauty shop every Friday, where she also had a weekly manicure. ("For an extra seven dollars," she once said, "I can be a lady.") She had a furrier and a jeweler. She wore Ferragamo shoes. Never in the least embarrassed by glitz, in later years she drove a deeply maroon Cadillac Seville. Once, when we were locked in by heavy traffic at O'Hare airport, I suggested my mother put her arm out the window in the hope of someone giving her a break and letting her back into the flow of cars. "Not likely," she said. "In this car, people figure I've already had my break."

That remark was characteristic of what I think my mother's realism. No one was less given to fantasy, idealism, nonsense than she. No one was less neurotic. If she ever felt anxiety, she never showed it in my presence. Nor did I ever see her depressed, until the very end of her life, when she was diagnosed with liver cancer. And here the depression took the form of surprise: "Whoever thought this would happen to me?" she said on more than one occasion.

She was never less than dutiful as a mother, providing meals, fresh laundry, an always immaculate apartment. What she never provided was advice. I remember once, I must have been eight or nine years old, telling my mother I was bored. "Oh," she said, "if you're bored, knock your head against the wall; it'll take your mind off your boredom." She might mildly reprimand me for not hanging up my clothes, but the reprimands never came close to nagging. I don't recall her ever telling me I needed a haircut or to be sure to wear my galoshes or anything else in the way of standard motherly advice.

The simple truth was that my brother and I were never at the center of my mother's or father's lives. When my brother and I were young, our parents would occasionally go off on vacations by themselves, leaving us in the care of professional babysitters—I recall one among them, a woman from the neighborhood named Charlotte Smucker—or of our childless Aunt Sally. I never felt any sense of deprivation or of being left behind when this occurred. Neither did I ever feel that either of my parents was in any way unfeeling or cold. Nor did I ever feel unloved. I knew, somehow, that if I needed my parents I could count on them. Parents of the day didn't, as they would later come to do, put the full-court press of attention on their children. At the same time, I cannot recall any of the parents of my friends or of neighbors who had been divorced.

My mother ceased working soon after her marriage, returning only in her late fifties to work in my father's business, where she kept the books and advised him, accurately, on whom among his customers he could safely advance credit. Before that she played cards with friends two, perhaps three times a week: poker, canasta, a game called kaluki, never bridge, the game of suburban Gentiles. My sense is that she usually won. "I took them," I remember her saying on one occasion, "like Grant took Richmond." She also attended luncheons given on behalf of charities. Owing to her husband's success in business, she was able to sponsor some of these luncheons herself: for the Jewish Home for the Blind, the Northwest Home for the Aged, the Cerebral Palsy Foundation. Sponsoring meant picking up the lunch tab for seventy or eighty women and paying for someone to do a dramatic reading or a singer who sounded like Barbra Streisand.

In the *Chicago Sun-Times* my mother read only the obituaries and stories about scandal. She assumed, in the best Chicago tradition, that all politicians were guilty until proven innocent, and she never heard of any proven innocent. Nor was she overly impressed by physicians, believing many of them in medicine chiefly for the money. Driving through certain neighborhoods in and around Chicago—Sauganash, the suburb of Kenilworth—she would quietly note, "It's restricted, you know." (Restricted, of course, against Jews.) She managed to say it in a way that implied, Who would want to live among such dreary, dull people anyway?

My mother loved language, and I sometimes think that whatever skill I have with words came through her. Of a card-playing friend with raucous children, she reported their mother's saying to them, "Fight nice." A neighbor, noting her own advancing age, once told my mother she was "no sprung chicken." Another neighbor, a Russian émigré, mentioned to her that, after her husband's death, the money in their estate was tied up not in escrow but in "egg roll." My mother never swore, but might say a person was "full of hops." I once heard her call a child walking about in a diaper "Orkey Cocker." Unnecessary tumult she denoted "roozhey-boozhey," an invention of hers, I believe.

I never heard my mother speak Yiddish, but she seemed to have wonderfully concise definitions for all Yiddish words. When I once asked her what a *grauber yung* was, she replied instanter, "an unlettered bore." A *dreikop*, she responded to another of my queries, "is a muddlehead." When I told her I thought a *Kuni Lemel* was a muddlehead, she responded, "Yes, but a *Kuni Lemel* is a sweet *dreikop.*"

Odd though it is to say so, I am less than sure what my mother thought of me. I am fairly certain that she never read any of my books or magazine articles. Once, when I called to tell her that a book of mine won a $5,000 prize from the *Chicago Tribune*, she said, "We get that junk in the mail all the time. I just throw it out." Another time during a phone conversation with her, I heard typing. "Mother, are you typing while talking to me?" She answered: "Why not? I don't need all my attention to carry on a conversation with you." Reaching her on the phone after I hadn't called her for four or five days, she began by saying, "Hello, stranger," which sounded like the beginning of a Jewish joke.

I have no memory of my parents ever teaching me table or other manners. I suppose I must have imitated them in dealing with knives and forks and napkins. On one occasion, taken out for dinner with other members of our family by an uncle of my father's, I, at age seven or eight, ordered a T-bone steak, which turned out to be so large that it drooped over all sides of the plate. A number of people at the table remarked on its gargantuan size. After dinner, on the ride home, my mother mildly upbraided me, telling me that, when taken to dinner by someone else, I must never order the most expensive item on the menu.

I never thought of my mother as cold or in any way distant, but I have no recollection of her ever kissing or hugging me. Nor did I feel the want of her kisses and hugs. But, then, I didn't need my mother smothering me with hugs and kisses and regularly telling me she loved me. I didn't need it because she often proved her love. Once, notably, when I went through a divorce from my first wife, having custody of my four children (two stepchildren and two of my own), my mother took charge of my two younger children, then eight and six years old, for a full school year, while I went through the complications of resettling my broken family in a new apartment in a new neighborhood. My mother was then in her sixties and never once complained of the substantial burden I had put on her, which she handled admirably.

My last strong memory of my mother is at her furrier's in Skokie. She was by then dying of cancer and wanted to give a parting gift of mink coats to her two daughters-in-law. While sifting through the various coats on display in the shop, my wife noted a handsome beaver coat. My mother, sitting erect in a nearby wing chair, said, more like announced, "Barbara, we are here to buy mink." Perfecto!

My parents' social life was almost entirely restricted to their extended family. The family of nieces, nephews, cousins at two or three removes was much more powerful in that day than in ours. I haven't spoken to any of my first cousins in several years, and what contact I have had with a few among them has been chiefly through email. But my parents traveled out to Roseland on the far

South Side of Chicago to visit my father's cousin Nelly Rosen and her husband, Joe. My mother's sisters and their children were regular visitors at our apartment and we at theirs for Jewish holidays and on other occasions. At one point, when my mother's youngest sister had a nervous breakdown and had to enter a mental asylum, my mother took in and raised her ten-year-old son for roughly five years; another sister raised her daughter during the same period. Family meant more sixty or so years ago than it does today.

Consider my own family. My brother, five and a half years younger than I, and someone I like very much, after serving six months in the Coast Guard married a woman from San Francisco and has lived in Northern California all his adult life. He is a better brother to me than I am to him; he never fails to call me on my birthday, and he responds to the various bits of my writing that I send him. Yet we have not seen each other for more than a decade. He has two children who, themselves, have now had children. I have never met any of these grand-nieces and -nephews, and know nothing about them, apart from the fact that one boy among them ran track at Dartmouth. I am not sure they even know of my existence. When I die, if they are even informed of my death, I imagine them responding by saying, "Really? . . . What's for dinner?" So much for the extended family in our time—it doesn't extend very far.

My father was ninety-two when he died, in his sleep, in his own apartment in Chicago. Such was the relentlessness of his vigor that, until his last years, I referred to him, behind his back of course, as the Energizer Bunny: he just kept going. I used to joke—half joke is closer to it—about "the vague possibility" that he might predecease me.

When an aged parent dies, one's feelings are greatly mixed. I was relieved that my father had what seems to have been an easeful death. In truth, I was also relieved at not having to worry about him any longer (though, apart from running certain errands and keeping his checkbook in the last few years of his life, he really gave my wife and me very little to worry about). But with him dead, I have been made acutely conscious that I am next in line for the guillotine: *C'est*, as Pascal would have it, *la condition humaine*.

Now that my father is gone, many questions will never be answered. Not long before he died I was driving him to his accountant's office and, without any transition, he said, "I wanted a third child, but your mother wasn't interested." This was the first I had heard about it. He was never a very engaged parent, certainly not by the full-court press standards of today. Having had two sons—me and my younger brother—had he, I suddenly wondered, begun to yearn for a daughter?

"Why wasn't Mother interested?" I asked. He didn't remember.

On another of our drives in that last year, he asked me if I had anything in the works in the way of business. I told him I had been invited to give a lecture at the University of Pennsylvania in Philadelphia. He inquired if there was a fee. I said there was a fee of $5,000.

"For an hour's talk?" he said, a look of curiosity on his face. "Fifty minutes, actually," I said, unable to resist provoking him lightly. His look changed from curiosity to astonishment. The country had to be in one hell of a sorry condition if they were passing out that kind of dough for mere talk from his son.

Was he a good father? This was the question an acquaintance not long ago put to me at lunch. When I asked what he meant by good, he said: "Was he, for example, fair?"

My father was completely fair, never showing the least favoritism between my brother and me (a judgment my brother has confirmed). He also set an example of decency, nicely qualified by realism. "No one is asking you to be an angel in this world," he told me when I was fourteen, "but that doesn't give you warrant to be a son of a bitch." And, as this suggests, he was an unrelenting fount of advice, some of it pretty obvious, none of it foolish. "Always put something by for a rainy day." "People know more about you than you think." "Work for a man for a dollar an hour—always give him at least a dollar and a quarter's effort."

Some of his advice seemed wildly misplaced. "Next to your brother, money's your best friend" was a remark made all the more unconvincing by the fact that my brother and I were never that close to begin with. On the subject of sex, the full extent of his wisdom was: "You want to be careful." Of what, exactly, was I to be careful—Venereal disease? Pregnancy? Getting entangled with the wrong girl?—he never filled in.

My father and I spent a lot of time together when I was an adolescent. He manufactured and imported costume jewelry and novelties—identification bracelets, pendants, cigarette lighters, miniature cameras, bolo ties—which he sold to Woolworth's, to the International Shoe Company, to banks, and to concessionaires at state fairs. I traveled with him in the summer to these fairs, spelling him at the wheel of his Buicks and Oldsmobiles, toting his sample cases, writing up orders, listening to him tell—ad infinitum, ad nauseam—the same three or four jokes to customers. We shared rooms in less-than-first-class hotels in midwestern towns—Des Moines, Minneapolis, Columbus—but never achieved anything close to intimacy, at least in our conversation.

His commercial advice was as useful to me as his advice about sex. "Always keep a low overhead." "You make your money in buying right, you know, not in selling." "Never run away from business." Some of it has stuck, however: nearly a half century later, I still find it hard to turn down a writing assignment, lest I prove guilty of running away from business.

My least favorite of my father's maxims was: "You can't argue with success." In my growing-up days, I thought there was nothing better to argue with. I tried to tell him why, but I never seemed to get my point across. The only time our arguments ever got close to the shouting stage, amusingly enough, was over the question of whether or not federal budgets had to be balanced. I was then in my twenties, and our ignorance on this question was equal and mutual—though he turned out to be right: all things considered, balanced is better.

When not in his homiletic mode, my father could be very penetrating. "There are three ways to do business in this country," he once told me. "At the top level you rely heavily on national advertising and public relations. At the next level, you take people out to dinner or golfing, you buy them theater tickets, supply women. And then there's my level." Pause. Asked what went on there, he replied: "I cut prices." His level, I thought then, and still think, much the most honorable.

He appreciated jokes, although in telling them he could barely sustain even a brief narrative. His own best wit entailed a comic resignation. In his late eighties, he made the mistake of sending to a great-nephew, whom he had never met, a bar mitzvah gift check for $1,000, instead of the $100 he had intended. When I discovered the error while going over his checkbook and pointed it out to him, he paused only briefly, smiled, and said, "Boy, is his younger brother going to be disappointed." At a certain point late in his business life he became intent on collecting even rather small debts owed him by deadbeat customers. "It's not the principle," he said. "It's the money."

Work was the place where my father seemed most alive, most impressive. Born in Montreal and having never finished high school, he came to America at seventeen, not long before the Depression. He took various flunky jobs, but soon found his niche as a salesman. "Kid," one of his bosses once told him, so good was he at his work, "try to remember that this desk I'm sitting behind is not for sale." Eventually, he owned his own small business.

He worked six days a week, usually arriving at 7:30 a.m. If he could find some excuse to go down to work on Sunday, he was delighted to do so. On his rare vacations, he would call in two or three times a day to find out what had come in the mail, who telephoned, what deliveries arrived. He never had more than eight or nine employees, but the business was fairly lucrative. In the late 1960s I recall him saying to me, "The country must be in terrible shape. You should see the crap I'm selling." Neither my brother nor I ever seriously thought about joining the business, sensing that it was a one-man show, without sufficient oxygen for two. In later years, a nephew worked for my father. One day, after he had had a falling-out with this nephew, my father said to me, "The kid's worked for me for fifteen years. We open at eight thirty, and for fifteen years he has come in at exactly eight thirty. You'd think once—just once—he'd be early."

"I call people rich," Henry James has Ralph Touchett say in *The Portrait of a Lady*, "when they're able to meet the requirements of their imagination." Although not immensely wealthy, my father made enough money fully to meet the demands of his. He could give ample sums to (mostly Jewish) charities, help out poor relatives, pay for his sons' education, buy his wife the diamonds and furs and good clothes that were among the trophies of my parents' generation, and in retirement take his grandsons to Israel, Africa, Asia, Latin America, the Soviet Union, Australia, New Zealand. At the very end, he told me that what most pleased him about his financial independence was never having to fall back on anyone else for help, right up to and including his exit from the world.

In my late twenties, my father, then in his late fifties, had a mild heart attack, and I feared I would lose him without ever getting to know him better. Having just recently returned to Chicago after a stint directing an anti-poverty program in Little Rock, Arkansas, I thought it might be a good thing if we were to meet once a week for lunch. On the first of these occasions, I took him to a French restaurant on the Near North Side. The lunch lasted nearly ninety minutes. I could practically smell his boredom, feel his longing to get back to "the place," as he called his business, then located on North Avenue just west of Damen. We never lunched alone again until after my mother's death, when I felt he needed company.

At some point—around, I think, the time he hit sixty—my father, like many another successful men operating within a fairly small circle, ceased listening. A courteous, even courtly man, he was, please understand, never rude. He would give you your turn and not interrupt, nodding his head in agreement at much of what you said. But he was merely waiting—waiting to insert one of his own thoughts. He had long since mastered the falsely modest introductory clause, which he put to regular use: "I'm inclined to believe that there is more good than bad in the world," he might offer, or "I may be mistaken, but don't you agree that disease and war are Mother Nature's way of thinning out the population?" I winced when I learned that the father of a friend of mine, having met him a few times, had taken to referring to my father as "the rabbi."

Although my father did not dwell on the past, neither was he much interested in the future. He had an astonishing ability to block things out, including his own illnesses, even surgeries. He claimed to have no memory of his heart attack, and he chose not to remember that, like many men past their mid-eighties, he had had prostate cancer. "I'm a great believer in mind over matter," he used to say, and so he applied his own mind over the matter of many details in his life.

He also liked to say that there wasn't anything really new under the sun. When I would report some excess to him—for example, a lunch check of $230 for two in New York—he would say: "What're ya, kidding me?" Although he was greatly interested in human nature, psychology at the level of the individual held no attraction for him. If I told him about someone's odd or unpredictable or stupid behavior, he would respond, "What is he, crazy?"

After his retirement at seventy-five, my father began to write. His own father had composed two books—one in Hebrew and one in Yiddish—for which my father had paid most of the expense of private publication. Offering to sell some of these books for his father, he kept a hundred or so copies stored in our basement. This turned out to be a ruse for increasing the monthly stipend he was already sending my grandfather: each month he would add $30, $45, or $50 to this stipend, saying it represented payment for books he had sold. Then one day a UPS truck pulled up with another hundred books and a note from my grandfather, saying he was worried that his son's stock was running low.

And now here was I, his eldest son, also publishing books. My father must have felt—with a heavy dose here of mutatis mutandis—like the Mendelssohn who was the son of the philosopher and the father of the composer, but never quite had his own shot at a touch of intellectual glory. So, as I noted, my father, too, began writing. His preferred form was the two- or three-sentence *pensée* (he would never have called it that), usually pointing a moral. "Man forces nature to reveal her chemical secrets" is an example of his work in this line. "Nature evens the score because man cannot always control the chemicals."

Often in the middle of the morning my phone would ring, and it would be my father with a question: "How do you spell 'affinity'?" Then he would ask if he was using the word correctly in the passage he was writing, which he would read to me. I always told him I thought his observations were interesting, or accurate, or that I had never before now thought of the point he was making. Often I tossed in minor corrections, or I might suggest that his second sentence didn't quite follow from his first. I loved him too much to say that a lot of what he had written bordered on the commonplace and, alas, sometimes crossed that border. I'm not sure he cared all that much about my opinion anyway.

He began to carry a small notepad in his shirt pocket. On his afternoon walks, new material would occur to him. Adding pages daily—hourly, almost—he announced one day that he had a manuscript of more than a thousand pages. He referred to these writings offhandedly as "my stuff," or "my crap," or "the *chazerai* I write." Still, he wanted to know what I thought about sending them to a publisher. The situation was quite hopeless; but I, lying, said it was worth a try, and wrote a letter over his name to accompany a packet of fifty or so pages of typescript. He began with the major publishers, then went to the larger university presses, then to more obscure places.

After ten or so rejections, I suggested a vanity press arrangement—never using the deadly word "vanity." For $5,000 or so, he could have five hundred copies of a moderate-size book printed for his posterity. But he had too much pride for that, and after a while he ceased to send out his material. What he was writing, he concluded, as he once put it to me, was "too hot" for the contemporary world. But he kept on scribbling away, flagging only in the last few years of his life, when he complained that his inspiration was drying up. Altogether he had ended up with some 2,700 pages—his earnest, ardent attempt to make sense of the world before departing it. While he had no more luck in this venture than the rest of us, there was, indisputably, something gallant about the attempt.

Becoming aware of our fathers' fallibilities is a jolt. When I was six years old, we lived in a neighborhood where I was the youngest kid on the block and thus prey to eight- and nine-year-olds with normal boyish bullying tendencies. One of them, a kid named Denny Price, was roughing me up one day when I told him that if he didn't stop, my father would get him. "Ya fadda," said Denny Price, "is an asshole." Even to hear my father spoken of this way sickened me. I would have preferred another punch in the stomach.

World War II was over by the time I was eight, but I remember being disappointed that my father had not gone off to fight. (He was too old and had children.) I also recall my embarrassment—I was

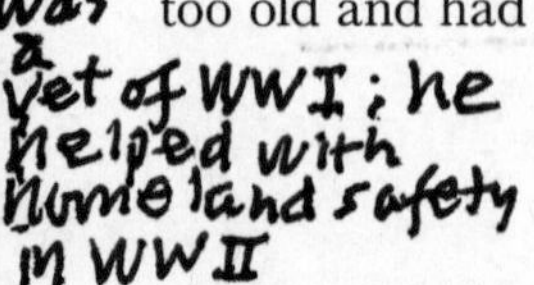

nine—at seeing him at an office party of a jewelry company he then worked for (called Beiler-Levine on Wabash Avenue), clownishly placing his hand on the stomach of a pregnant secretary, closing his eyes, and predicting the sex of the child.

He was less stylish than many of my friends' fathers. When he went to the beach (which he rarely did), he marched down in black business shoes, socks with clocks on them, and very white legs. He cared not at all about sports—which, when I was young, was the only thing I did care about. Later, I saw him come to wrong decisions about real estate, worry in a fidgeting way over small sums he was owed, make serious misjudgments about people. He preferred to operate, rather as in his writing, at too high a level of generality. "Mother Nature abhors a vacuum," he used to say, and I, to myself, would think, "No, Dad, it's a vacuum cleaner salesman she abhors." At some point in my thirties I concluded that my father was not nearly so subtle or penetrating as my mother.

What do boys and young men want from their fathers? For the most part I think we want precisely what they cannot give us—a painless transfusion of wisdom, a key to life's mysteries, the secret to happiness, assurance that one's daily struggles and aggravations amount to something more than some stupid cosmic joke with no punch line. Oh, Dad, you have been here longer than I, you have been in the trenches, up and over the hill; quick, before you exit, fill me in: Does it all add up, cohere, make any sense at all, what's the true story, the real *emes*, tell me, please, Dad? By the time my father reached sixty, I knew he could not deliver any of this.

Now, past eighty myself, I cannot say I can do much better. Besides, the virtues my father did have, and did deliver on, were impressive.

Steadfastness was high on the list. He was a man you could count on. He saw my mother through a three-year losing struggle against cancer, doing the shopping, the laundry, even some of the cooking, trying to keep up her spirits, never letting his own spirits fall. He called himself a realist, but he was in fact a sentimentalist, with a special weakness, in his later years, for his extended family. (He and his twin brother were the youngest of ten children, eight boys and two girls, my father being the only financial success among them.) He had great reverence for his own father, always repeating his sayings, marveling at his wisdom.

My brother and I may not have reverenced our father, but we certainly paid him obeisance. His was the last generation of fathers to draw off the old Roman authority of the paterfamilias. The least tyrannical of men, my father was nevertheless accorded a high level of service at home because of his role as head of the household and efficient breadwinner. Dinner always awaited his return from work. One did not open the evening paper until he had gone through it first. "Get your father a glass of water," my mother would say, or "Get your father his slippers," and my brother and I would do so without quibble. A grandfather now myself, I have never received, nor ever expect to receive, any of these little services.

My father lived comfortably with his contradictions—another great virtue, I think. He called himself an agnostic, for example, and belonged to no synagogue, yet it was clear that he would have been greatly disappointed had any of his grandsons not had a bris and later a bar mitzvah. He gave large sums to Jewish charities, and at one point put upon the wall of his den a plaque from the Israel Bonds Office in Chicago that read "Morese Epstein, $25,000 Donor." When

I pointed out that they had misspelled his first name of Maurice, he replied, "You can't really expect them to spell your name correctly for less than a hundred-thousand-dollar donation." So exulted was he over the successful Israeli counterterrorist raid at the Entebbe airport in Uganda in 1976 that he donated the cost of an ambulance to the Israeli Red Cross.

Only the Jews, as far as I know, are able to live with such contradictions, ignoring their religion, yet adhering to the culture of their coreligionists. One is reminded of the joke about a Jew from a shtetl who visits Warsaw. Upon return, he tells his friend of the wonders he had seen:

"I met a Jew who had grown up in a yeshiva and knew large portions of the Talmud by heart. I met a Jew who was an atheist. I met a Jew who owned a large clothing store with many employees, and I met a Jew who was an ardent communist."

"What's so strange?" his friend asks. "Warsaw is a big city. Nearly a million Jews live there."

"You do not understand," the man answers, "it was the same Jew."

My father always invoked the soundness of business principles, yet in cases of the least conflict between these principles and a generous impulse, he would inevitably act on the latter: loaning money to the wrong people, giving breaks to men who did not seem to deserve them, helping out financially whenever called upon to do so. To bums stopping him for a handout he used to say, "Beat it. I'm working this side of the street," yet he gave his old suits and overcoats to a poor brain-fozzled alcoholic who slept in the doorways on North Avenue near his place of business.

Whether out of lack of interest or by plan, my father allowed me to make nearly all my own decisions. True, he had insisted that I go to Hebrew school, on the grounds, often repeated, that "a Jew should know something of his background, about where he comes from." But apart from that, my brother and I decided what we would study, where we would go to college, and with whom. He never told me what kind of work to go into, offering only another of his much-repeated and in this instance true apothegms: "You've got to love your work." He never told me what to do with my money. He let me go absolutely my own way.

Only now does it occur to me that I never sought my father's approval; growing up, I mainly tried to avoid his disapproval so that I could retain the large domain of freedom he permitted me. For starters, he was unqualified to dispense approval where I sought it: for my athletic prowess when young; for my intellectual work when older. Then, too, artificially building up his sons' confidence through a steady stream of heavy and continuous approval—the modus opeandi of many contemporary parents—was not his style. "You handled that in a very businesslike way," my father once told me about some small matter I had arranged for him, but I cannot recall his otherwise praising me. I would send him published copies of things I wrote, and he would read them, usually confining his response to "very interesting" or remarking on how something I said had suggested a thought of his own.

In my middle thirties I was offered a job teaching at nearby Northwestern University. In balancing the debits and credits of the offer, I mentioned to my father that the job would allow me to spend more time with my two sons. "I don't mean to butt in," he said, before proceeding to deliver one of the longer speeches of his paternal career, "but that sounds to me like a load of crap. If you're going to take a teaching job, take it because you want to teach, or because you can use the extra time for other work, not because of your kids. Con yourself into thinking you make decisions because of your children and you'll end up one of those pathetic old guys whining about his children's ingratitude. Your responsibilities to your sons include feeding them and seeing they have a decent place to live and helping them get the best schooling they're capable of and teaching them right from wrong and making it clear they can come to you if they're in trouble and setting them an example of how a man should live. That's how I looked upon my responsibility to you and your brother. But for a man, work comes first."

In the raising of my sons, I attempted, roughly, to imitate my father—but already the historical moment for confidence of the kind he had brought to fatherhood was past. For one thing, I was a divorced father (though with custody of my sons), so I had already done something to them that my father never did to me—break up their family. For another, I found myself regularly telling my sons that I loved them. I told them this so often that they probably came to doubt it.

True, I wasn't like one of those fathers who these days show up for all their children's school activities, driving them to four or five different kinds of lessons, making a complete videotaped record of their first eighteen years, taking them to lots of ball games, art galleries, and (ultimately, no doubt) the therapist. But I was, nonetheless, plenty nervous in the service, wondering if I were doing the right thing, never really confident I was a good enough—or even adequate—father. The generation of fathers now raising children,

I sense, is even more nervous than I was then, and the service itself, has become a full-time job.

Many are the kinds of bad luck one can have in a father. Being the son of certain men—I think here of Alger Hiss's son, Tony, who seems to have devoted so much of his life to defending his father's reputation—can absorb all of one's life. One can have a father whose success is so great as to stunt one's own ambition, or a father whose failure has so embittered him as to leave one with permanently bleak views and an overwhelmingly dark, in Henry James's phrase, "imagination of disaster." Having too strong a father can be a problem, but so can having too weak a father. A father may desert his family and always leave one in doubt, or a father may commit suicide and leave one in a despair much darker and deeper than any normal doubt. Worst luck of all, perhaps, is to have one's father die of illness or accident before one has even known him.

"They fuck you up, your mum and dad," wrote Philip Larkin. "They may not mean to, but they do. / They fill you with the faults they had / And add some extra, just for you." This perhaps best-known quatrain in modern poetry is not only amusing but, some would argue, true. But need it be true? Ought one to blame one's parents for all that one (disappointingly) is, or that one (equally disappointingly) has never become? One of the most successful men I know once told me, without the least passion in his voice, "Actually, I dislike my parents quite a bit"—which didn't stop him, when his parents were alive, from being a dutiful son. (We are, after all, commanded to honor our parents, not necessarily to love them.) Taking the heat off parents for the full responsibility for the fate of their children throws the responsibility back on oneself, where it almost always belongs.

The best luck is, of course, to love one's parents without complication, which has been my fortunate lot. Whether consciously or not—I cannot be certain even now—my parents gave me the greatest gift of all. By leaving me alone, while somehow never leaving me in doubt that I could count on them when needed, they gave me the freedom to go my own way and to become myself. To the almost cripplingly excessive concern for the proper rearing of children in our own day, in all its fussiness and fear, my father's response, I'm almost certain, would have been: "What're they, crazy?"

Chapter Three

What's in a Name?

My grandmother's maid, Minnie Tumbletee, once told me that I was my grandmother's favorite grandchild. She, my grandmother, wanted to have me named Adrian, perhaps after herself, whose name was Ada. Adrian, an androgynous name in England, was and remains in America largely taken as feminine, and would doubtless have caused me much grief growing up in Chicago, rather in the manner of Johnny Cash's "A Boy Named Sue." My mother instead named me Myron Joseph. Myron after whom I do not know, Joseph after one of my father's earlier employers, a man he admired and felt grateful to, named Joseph Sternberg.

Along with many other things I neglected to ask my mother when she was alive—Did she believe in God? How did she meet my father? From where in Europe did her family derive before turning up in England?—was Why Myron? The name is Greek, at least there was the Greek sculptor Myron (c. 470–430 BC), a Myron who was a historian and rhetorician turns up in the third century BC, and Thucydides mentions a figure named "Myron the accuser." The abrasive journalist Mike Wallace was another Myron. I have to assume that my mother was taken by the false elegance of the name. So many Jewish mothers of my mother's generation named their sons as if they were English hotels: Seymour, Howard, Norman, Harvey, Ronald, Arnold, Sheldon, etc. Myron was in any case never a name that seemed to me a comfortable fit.

Throughout my boyhood I was known as Mike, with only schoolteachers, the Social Security Administration, and the U.S. Army referring to me as Myron. People who know me from the old country, as I think of my boyhood in the far North Side neighborhood of Chicago known as West Rogers Park, still think of me as—and some still call me—Mike. But to my wife and other close friends I am Joe, or Joseph, the name I used when I first published an article in the *New Leader* in 1959 at the age of twenty-two.

I did a further bit of nomenclatorplasty on my last name, pronouncing it Ep*stine* instead of Epsteen, as most people with a steinly suffix to their names tend to do. The history of this stine-steen business, I believe, goes back to World War I, when anti-German feeling in America ran high, and many stines, to avoid seeming in the least German, steened themselves. I prefer Epstine not only because it is a return to origin but because it sounds more frankly Jewish.

Henry James claimed to have memories going back to his second year, recollecting sitting in his Aunt Kate's lap in a carriage passing the Place Vendôme in Paris in 1844. The furthest I can go back is a blurry memory of my own toilet training, being congratulated for using a toilet to urinate, standing there, "mecky," as I was told by my grandmother to refer to my infant member, in hand. I also have an early memory of being allowed to eat a vast quantity of ice cream in a hospital bed after having had my tonsils removed, another of those medical fashions visited upon my generation of children, now gone by the boards.

But my first distinct memories are those of living with my parents, my brother not yet born, in a furnished apartment in the Pratt Lane Hotel, a block or so from Lake Michigan in Rogers Park. I can recall the lobby, the switchboard, a few of my parents' friends who also lived at the Pratt Lane. An older boy living in the building named Arnold was especially kind to me, and when my mother told me that I now had a baby brother and asked me what I thought I should name him, I said, "Arnold," which she did. Apologies, bro.

We must have still been living at the Pratt Lane when the United States entered World War II. I remember singing there for my parents and their friends "Any Bonds Today?" ("Bonds of freedom / That's what I'm selling / Any bonds today?") This was, of course, the last war that the country was fully behind. For one thing, we were attacked at Pearl Harbor and, for another, everyone had or knew someone fighting in the war—relatives, friends, neighbors. The war, our great war, suffused all of American life.

I was five years old when we joined the Allies and eight when the war was over. I recall saving newspapers and my mother saving grease in cans for the war effort. At Eugene Field Grammar School we bought war stamps, for, I believe, a dime a piece. We also had occasional air-raid drills, during which we were marched off to the school's basement. In the schoolyard, we chanted, "Whistle while you work, Hitler is a jerk, Mussolini is a meany, and the Japs are worse." No new cars were produced during the war and our family car was a 1941 green Dodge sedan. Rationing of food and gasoline didn't affect me directly—after all, I then knew no other world than that of rationing—though not long after the war was over someone announced that a local candy store was selling Fleer's bubble gum, unavailable through the war, and I remember standing in line to buy mine (limited to one piece to a customer). The newsreels then shown at all movies were chiefly about the war. If we passed a serviceman in uniform hitchhiking, my father without hesitation would stop to pick him up. The country was never so unified in my lifetime as it was during this war.

During World War II and for long after, my father would not allow the *Chicago Tribune* in the house. His argument was with the paper's, or at least with its publisher Robert McCormick's, isolationist policy before the war. (I regretted this because the *Tribune* had *Dick Tracy* and other of the best newspaper comics.) My father recounted the story how, one day, just off Chicago's Outer Drive, he had a flat tire and a *Chicago Tribune* truck driver pulled up to help him. My father told him to get the hell away, he didn't want any help from anyone connected with the goddamned *Trib.* "That just goes to show," my father ended this anecdote by saying, "how stupid politics can make you."

Just before the end of the war our family moved to a one-bedroom apartment in a brown courtyard building at 7023 North Sheridan Road. To begin with some rather pathetic, secondary name-dropping, across from us in the same courtyard lived with her husband a woman named Ida Kaplan, the sister of Barney Ross, former lightweight, light-welterweight, and welterweight boxing champion of the world. Down below lived the Glicks, cousins to the comedian Morey Amsterdam.

In the courtyard building to the north lived the Libby brothers, Pete and Sam, and their wives and children. The brothers had small hamburger joints round the city. Pete was much the flashier of the two brothers, and years later, after his wife had died, one night on Rush Street, Chicago's nightclub district, I saw him slowly driving a red Cadillac convertible, the singer Patti Page riding shotgun beside him. Jack Libby, a few years older than I, was the son of Sam Libby, and a boy I much admired, who always went out of his way to include me in games with other neighborhood kids. His mother, Sarah, went to Marshall High School with my mother.

In the same building as the Libbys lived the Cowlings. The father, Sam Cowling, was the comedian on the then immensely popular radio show *Don McNeill's Breakfast Club.* Dale was his wife's name, the same name as Roy Rogers's wife; and their two children were Sam Jr. and Billy. The Cowlings were Catholic, and they seemed to me admirably—even enviably—as American as one could be. Both Sam Jr. and Billy went to St. Jerome's, then Loyola Academy, thence to Catholic Georgetown University.

In those days I thought Catholicism coterminous with Christianity. This was the time of what seemed the endless Bing Crosby–Barry Fitzgerald–Pat O'Brien priestly flicks (*Going My Way, The Bells of St. Mary's*, etc.). With its large Polish, Italian, Irish populations, Chicago was a very Catholic city, and everywhere in its streets, on its buses, subways, streetcars one encountered nuns in full habit—not as now, the habit kicked, in pantsuits—and priests in clerical collars. The Church was strong enough to insist that men and women not themselves Catholics who married Catholics sign a document agreeing that any children in the marriage be raised Catholic. In a self-imposed segregation, kids who went to Catholic schools did not mix often or easily with kids who went to public schools. A Catholic friend not long ago told me that when he was a boy he was instructed not to go into the YMCA, where they might attempt to convert him.

One night, returning with my father from the 400 movie theater after seeing what must have been a movie in which Bing Crosby played yet another priest, I asked if we could have a Christmas tree. "No," my father said. When I ask why, he told me that we were Jews, and Jews didn't have Christmas trees. Case closed. I didn't get it, but what I did get was that, as a Jew, I was somehow different, somehow maybe not quite fully American. Only years later did I come to realize that Judaism, along with being one of the world's oldest religions, was a very superior club, one whose members over the centuries survived the most vicious persecutions, while accounting for some of the world's most impressive scientific, artistic, and intellectual achievements—a club in which I was more than delighted to be a member. Yet one evening, sitting in the Henry Crown Hall in Jerusalem, awaiting the arrival of the Jerusalem Symphony Orchestra, I looked about and thought how everyone in that room might well be Jewish, when I, somehow, preferred being in a minority.

The courtyard on Sheridan Road had a life of its own. Hurdy-gurdy men would occasionally appear, some with monkeys, and housewives would toss coins wrapped in bits of newspaper down to them. One warm Sunday evening my father sent me to West's Pharmacy at the corner of Sheridan and Lunt for three Perfecto Garcia cigars (twenty-five cents each), and on the way back, most of the windows in the courtyard apartments being open in this, the age before air-conditioning, I heard twenty-five or so radios all playing *The Jack Benny Program* as if in unison.

My parents gave the bedroom in their one-bedroom apartment over to me and my then baby brother, so that they could meet friends at night in their living room, where they slept on a foldout couch. Sitting on this couch, my father read stories to me out of a children's Old Testament and *The Adventures of Robin Hood.* He also set me sums to add up and bought me a pair of boxing gloves. "Never be afraid of bullies," he instructed me as he taught me to keep my guard up, how to jab, throw hooks and uppercuts. "Remember," he told me, "the bigger they are, the harder they fall." This last being perhaps the platitude with the lowest truth quotient of any ever uttered.

At night I would sit at the window of my brother's and my bedroom counting the steady stream of cars passing below on Sheridan Road. I told myself I would go to bed only after, say, ten Packards or fifteen DeSotos had passed. Knowing the makes of cars, identifiable by their grilles, was my first form of organized knowledge. Learning arithmetic through computing baseball batting averages was my second.

Behind our building was a park and behind that Lake Michigan. Sullivan High School's football team practiced in the park, and I would spend parts of my afternoons watching its workouts and its coach, a chesty gent named Ralph Margolis, yell, "*Schtunk!*" at erring players. (This being much preferred to the Chicago Bears coach George Halas's regular imprecation of "cocksucker.") In the early evenings kids from around the block gathered to play kick the can, capture the flag, red rover, and other games. I was among the youngest of these kids, and hence without much in the way of status. In choose-up sports—ours was the last generation before Little League, or other adult-organized play—I was among the last chosen and then assigned such hopeless positions as center in football or right fielder in baseball. Nor did it help that the early years of school bored me blue. I seemed to be someone who excelled nowhere. Owing to all this I did not have an especially high opinion of myself. I couldn't in fact quite see my significance, if I had any at all.

At eight years old, I was sent off to an eight-week session of summer camp in Eagle River, Wisconsin. The camp was called Interlaken (not to be confused, which it often was, with the music camp of a similar name). Coach Margolis was one of the camp's directors. I learned two things over those eight weeks: how to make lanyards and how to use profanity. Before Camp Interlaken, I said gosh and golly, cry peet and cripes, heck, darn, and phooey; after Interlaken I had a full arsenal of four-letter and other choice words at my command, the least offensive of which were hell, damn, and crap. I never returned for a second summer at Eagle River.

Ours was the last generation of boys to wear knickers, trousers that ended with elastic bands at the knees, with long socks below them. I remember owning a particularly ugly pair made of corduroy meant to resemble tweed and called tweeduroy. Blue jeans had not yet come into fashion. The only denim trousers available were called dungarees and thought fit only for farmers. (To be called a farmer, in those days, implied one was without sophistication, a simpleton.) As a young boy, I remember wishing for long pants, but had to wait until I was nine years old before I was allowed to wear them.

When I was ten years old, in 1947, my parents bought a two-flat apartment building on Campbell Avenue in West Rogers Park for what now seems the impressively low price of $14,000. The neighborhood was chiefly given over to two-, three-, and six-flat buildings, with a sprinkling of bungalows among them. We occupied the first floor; a childless couple named the Andersons, with Mrs. Anderson's unmarried sister, Edna, lived on the second. I was assigned to mow the lawn and shovel the snow. The first time I mowed our small lawn, I called my father out to approve my work. He looked about, pointed out the spots I missed, and announced: "The next time there is a Depression, it's guys like you they'll let go first."

The West Rogers Park neighborhood was changing, and we Jews were the cause of its change. The hub of West Rogers Park was Devon Avenue (pronounced "*Dee*-von," heavy accent on the first syllable), its main shopping drag. Over the next decade the street became more and more Judenized. Within seven blocks, it had four delis and three Chinese restaurants. (Ah, Chinese, the food of our people!) Adem & Dess and Turner Bros. were two excellent men's clothing stores, with the former always supplying impressive color-coordinated windows. A boys' clothing store called Little Men's Shop opened. Manzelmann Hardware supplied all household needs. Soon after, a sporting goods store called Pro Sport appeared in which the Chicago Cubs pitcher Johnny Klippstein worked. Not one but two five-and-ten-cent shops, Kresge's and Nisner's, were on Devon; so, too, two small department stores, Crawford's and Anderson's. A shop called Hobbymodels anchored the busy corner of Devon and Western Avenue. My mother sometimes shopped at Seymour Paisin, where they served customers cocktails in the afternoon. A food market on Devon called Hillman's was a precursor of the Whole Foods of our day.

The move to West Rogers changed me, too. In fact, it marked the first turning point in my life. With my transfer, in the fifth grade, from Eugene Field to Daniel Boone School, I suddenly became a star on the playground, the place it most mattered, perhaps the only place it mattered. I was always well coordinated, and I was adept at mimicking pro athletes. Now, suddenly, playing with kids my own age, I came in from right field to play shortstop; I left the position of center (as in "dunk the center") to become a T-formation quarterback. When, two or so years later, we took up basketball, I was a point guard. I am not sure how all this came about, but for the first time in my life I sensed I was genuinely liked by my peers, popular, a figure of significance. At his first school, Christ's Hospital, Charles Lamb was selected to be among a small clutch of the brightest boys, known as the deputy Grecians. Later Lamb wrote: "I don't know how it is, but I keep my rank in fancy still since school days. I can never forget that I was a deputy Grecian!" Nor can I forget that I was once a quarterback and a shortstop and a point guard.

Star on the playground I might have been, but not the brightest star. That would have been a boy six months younger than I named Marty Sommerfield. Marty was, like me, smallish, but, unlike me, or for that matter unlike anyone else I knew, absolutely fearless. He would crash into walls to catch fly balls. In football he played running back without a helmet. (In later life he wouldn't back down from fights with guys sixty or seventy pounds heavier than he.) He had a chipped front tooth, which on him looked good, admirable even. He had scientific interests, and in the basement of his family's bungalow on Coyle Avenue he dissected frogs and kept mice for experiments. He would go on to Evanston Township High School, on whose baseball team he played and at which he won a Westinghouse prize for a scientific project on enzymes. The prize gave him a scholarship to Swarthmore College, at which, one day in his sophomore year, he dynamited a three-hundred-year-old oak tree, for which he was kicked out of school. Marty's was a storied life. At one point he was arrested for burglary; he later dropped by Ann Arbor to pick up a doctorate in mathematics; he spent some time with Albert Schweitzer in Africa and afterward walked about with a pet monkey; he ended up teaching in Southeast Asia; and when it was discovered he had a hopeless cancer, he, his physical courage never having deserted him, took his own life.

My memory of these West Rogers Park years remains vivid. I cannot, for example, recall the names of any of my teachers during my first five years at Eugene Field School, and those of only a few of my classmates. But I have distinct memories of all my teachers at Boone School, those well-postured spinsters, Miss Schone, Miss Nihil, Miss Shure; the anomalous one male among them, the handsome math teacher Mr. Coleman Deans; later two beautiful younger women teachers, Miss Mandlestam and Miss Byrnes.

In the classroom, owing to two boys, David Netboy and Peter Lenn, who were quicker and cleverer, I discovered that I was no math genius. We were also taught Chicago history, leaving out its main elements of crime and corruption. Much time was devoted to handwriting and music (where I wished to sing bass, but was a natural alto). I remember a spelling bee in which everyone in the room had to sit down disqualified because no one could spell the word "Negro," all of us neglecting to capitalize the *N*. How the world has changed! Now one is not allowed to use the word "Negro," once a term of great dignity, and the name of Daniel Boone Elementary School has been changed to the Mosaic School of Fine Arts because it was revealed that Daniel Boone, the great American pioneer, kept slaves and lived on Indian land. Progress? Your call.

Culture had no place in those years in West Rogers Park. None of the boys among us took piano or violin lessons. Nor did being a good student count for much. The vaunted Jewish interest in politics and ideas counted for little not merely among us but among those of our parents whom I knew. Our parents were chiefly interested in making a good living, providing well for their families, gettin' on.

Jews of that day tended to divide into three strains: the seriously religious, the left-wing political, and the petit (or not so petit) bourgeois interested in the upward climb American life promised the diligent and hardworking. My friends and I and our parents were chiefly of the last camp. Doubtless we, like our parents, missed out on a lot; at the same time, we grew up with a feeling for reality perhaps not available to the political blinkered by their idealism or the religious humbled by their theology.

Four days a week after grammar school, I went off for an hour-long session of Hebrew school, which I did between the ages of ten and my bar mitzvah at thirteen. A great waste of time, this, since we were never taught to translate from Hebrew into English, but instead merely learned pronunciation of Hebrew vowels and consonants and a handful of prayers, concentrating during our final year on that small portion of the Torah that we read aloud from the bimah, or altar, a portion of rarely more than fifty lines. My own bar mitzvah party was held at the Ridgeview Hotel in Evanston, under the supervision of a stout middle-aged woman known as the Duchess, who arranged for the caterer and the small band of musicians and who forced everyone to sing "The Old Gray Mare" and dance the Mexican hat dance. The Ridgeview still stands and is now a halfway house for the insane. During the Duchess's days, I think of it as a full-way house.

Saturdays during these years we all went to the movies, chiefly to the Nortown Theater on Western Avenue, though occasionally to the Ciné on Devon and less often (an El ride) to the Biograph on Lincoln Avenue, before which John Dillinger was shot in 1934 by the police. We rarely inquired what was playing. We didn't have to. The late 1940s was a grand era for movies. All the great movie stars were at work, many at the top of their game: Humphrey Bogart and Fred Astaire, Myrna Loy and Barbara Stanwyck, John Wayne and Jimmy Stewart, Katharine Hepburn and Deborah Kerr, Jimmy Cagney and Spencer Tracy, Rosalind Russell and Bette Davis, and one could go on and on. I recently came upon the useful distinction between actors and stars: actors took on different roles, stars always played themselves. My boyhood was the age of stars.

The movies themselves were not yet intent on acquiring the second- and third-rate seriousness they later went in for, but content to tell a good, often a charming story, often ending in a lengthy kiss. The full program at the Nortown included two feature films, a cartoon, a newsreel, and coming attractions. Fifteen cents got one into the theater with enough left over for a box of popcorn and candy (my own favorite was a confection called Jujyfruits). I still remember the odd sensation of entering the Nortown on winter Saturdays at 1:00 p.m. and emerging at 5:00 p.m. into the darkened street.

Not all Saturdays, however, for in my last year in grammar school, along with several of my friends, I enrolled in something called Fortnightly, which was a ballroom-dancing class that met on Saturday afternoons in the field house of nearby Indian Boundary Park. I'm not sure why it was called Fortnightly, since I believe it met weekly, but the idea behind it was to inaugurate us young ruffians into the middle class by teaching us to waltz, fox-trot, rhumba, samba, and more. "Young gentlemen will now rise and invite young ladies to dance," the woman who led the program would call out. And so we did. Some of us young gentlemen met before Fortnightly at my parents' apartment, which was en route to Indian Boundary, to play, with neckties loosened, an hour or so of penny poker.

Summer months I walked the four blocks from our apartment to the Boone schoolyard, always finding other kids there ready to play baseball, either hardball or the Chicago version of softball, which entailed a sixteen-inch ball and no gloves. If there were not enough kids, we played no right-field hitting, and fewer still, we eliminated the first baseman and played pitcher's hands out. In the autumn, we had football practice at Chippewa Park, preparing for playing against the teams of nearby Clinton, Stone, Rogers, and St. Tim's schools.

Preoccupied with sports, I did not do much reading. What I did read, with passionate intensity, was a magazine called *Sport*. I read it with perhaps as much pleasure as any publication has ever given me. *Sport*, edited in that day by a man named Al (not Allen or Albert) Silverman, featured profiles of living athletes—"In the off-season, Yogi likes plenty of pizza, and can be found hanging out at his friend Phil Rizzuto's bowling alley"—and articles on such historical figures as Ty Cobb, Jim Thorpe, Babe Ruth, Man o' War. Each issue contained, toward its front, a *Sport* Quiz, the only quiz on which I ever really wished to do well. A new issue of the magazine was in the nature of an occasion. In later years, I was asked to write for *Sport*; to do an article on a now-forgotten (at least by me) Cleveland Browns running back for which I was to be paid the fee of $500. Alas, I turned the offer down; "alas" because I should have liked even now to think myself a contributor to *Sport*.

Sports allow kids a chance to develop competence and experience the pleasure it gives. I still cannot forget one lightly rainy day alone shooting baskets on a netless hoop on Talman Avenue just off Pratt, when I taught myself the hook shot. Somehow I quickly grasped the rhythm of the shot and—bang, bang, bang—hook after hook went in. The rain grew heavier, but I didn't want to leave that basket, and stayed out there for more than an hour more, drenched but delighted in my (generally useless) prowess with the hook.

My father allowed me to put up a basket with a wooden backboard in our backyard, and nearly every day from the age of twelve to fifteen I shot, underhand, a hundred free throws. My last year in grammar school I won a free throw–shooting contest at Green Briar Park, making twenty-three of twenty-five shots. I later played on the frosh-soph team in high school, but was too small to make the varsity.

That same year I began to play tennis, which was to become my main athletic passion through high school. I began playing on the cement courts of Indian Boundary Park, then one day went off to Evanston to play on the brown-clay courts at Northwestern University. After going back there three or four times, I was offered the job of ball boy for the pro, an amiable heavyset man named Paul Bennett. The job entailed rounding up balls hit during his lessons, and then soon after demonstrating the strokes and serves that Mr. Bennett taught, and which I had learned on the job. The job paid seventy-five cents an hour, with a 10 percent discount on clothes and equipment, and free use of the courts when I wasn't working with Mr. Bennett. I never had a better job.

As for the quality of my tennis, it was more stylish than effective. (Is the same, I wonder, true today of my prose?) In tan Fred Perry shorts, a white Lacoste shirt, Jack Purcell shoes, and the smoothest of smooth strokes pocking off my Jake Kramer racquet, I looked rather better than I played; or, put another way, I preferred looking good over winning. I lettered in tennis in high school, though I never rose higher than the doubles team. Along with a friend named Bob Swenson, we won the Chicago high school doubles championship. In the finals we beat a team from Fenger High School on the city's far South Side, whose players wore gym shoes and black socks. (The better tennis players in those years came from the suburbs and took lessons as early as five or six years old.) Among the short list of petty regrets in my life, I wish that as a boy I had concentrated less on style and more on winning tennis.

My parents never saw me play. I'm not sure that they even knew I did. I say this not out of resentment but instead in wonderment at the freedom from their supervision allowed me and most boys of my generation at that time. Only one father of the boys I knew bothered to come out to watch his son play softball. A flawed Latinist among us referred to him, the father, as *omnipresent*—it should have been *semperpresent*—a comic, even a pathetic, figure who had time to waste watching kids play games.

My father had two friends from his own boyhood in Montreal, the brothers Danny and Sammy Spunt, who owned and ran the Ringside Gym in the Loop, a training site for professional boxers.

When I was eleven my father took me along to visit the Spunts, who invited me to come back whenever I pleased.

I pleased fairly often. At eleven I took the Chicago El from West Rogers Park to the Loop, and hung around the gym, stimulated by the noise of punching bags, the spectacle of sparring boxers, even the smell of the place. Danny Spunt, the more agreeable of the two brothers, led me to a file case in which he kept eight-by-ten photographs of all the boxers of the day, and told me to help myself to any I wanted. I recall taking home photos of Sugar Ray Robinson, Kid Gavilan, Joe Louis, Gus Lesnevich, Jake LaMotta, Carmen Basilio, Billy Conn, and Johnny Bratton. Bratton, who would briefly become the welterweight champ in 1951, trained at Ringside. So did Tony Zale. One day Danny Spunt took me into the gym's locker room, where sat Zale, naked but for a leather Everlast jock. "Kid," said Danny, "I want you to meet Tony Zale, middleweight champion of the world." Zale looked up. "Hi, kid," he said. "Hi, Champ," I replied in what seemed to me an unnaturally high voice.

I suspect not many eleven-year-old boys or girls take the El in Chicago today, out of the reasonable fear on the part of their parents of their being robbed, molested, and worse. But the world of that day was a quieter, more settled, less frightful world. I knew of no children or parents who might be seeing a psychotherapist. Not yet fourteen, I remember in late autumn returning home from football practice at Chippewa Park, in my shoulder pads and orange-and-black team jersey, and in the darkening evening sighting several fires of burning leaves along the curbside gutter of Campbell Avenue and thinking how beautiful it, and the world I knew with it, all was.

Chapter Four

Not Your Good Ole Golden Rule Days

Studying in high school would only have detracted from the unrelenting good time I had during those four years. With one exception, that of geometry, I have no recollection of ever having brought a book home for study. No teacher ever saw the least promise in me, for I never provided any. Upon leaving grammar school, the question arose about what foreign language one should take in high school. Latin was suggested for brighter students. Students with scientific interests sometimes took German. Many girls took French. No suggestions were made for me, and so I wound up taking Spanish. (*El burro es un animal importante*, right?) Throughout high school, if I had heard a teacher was tough, I steered clear of him or her. Apart from gym, I rarely received a grade above a C. In my February graduating class, I finished 169 out of 213 students, just above the lower quarter.

Nicholas Senn High School, on Chicago's North Side, had roughly three thousand students. Among its small number of distinguished alumni have been the film directors William Friedkin and Philip Kaufman (a good friend of mine), the actors Barbara Harris, Harvey Korman, and Clayton Moore (who played the Lone Ranger), the singer Anita O'Day, the architect Stanley Tigerman, the novelists William Maxwell and John Jakes, and a puppeteer named Burr Tillstrom (the creator of Kukla, Fran, and Ollie). In *The Folded Leaf*, William Maxwell wrote a splendid novel with Senn High School as its background. Nicholas Senn (1844–1908) was a surgeon and medical researcher.

The school was, by my rough reckoning, 60 percent Jewish, 40 percent Gentile. When I went there in the early 1950s there were never more than three or four Black kids and no Hispanic kids that I can recall. The Jewish kids tended to come mostly from lower-middle- and middle-class families on the ascendant, the Gentile kids largely from working-class families. Segregation between Jews and Gentiles, while not complete, was nearly so. Only in sports was there genuine mixture between the two. Not that there was any open antagonism, nor the least hint of rivalrousness between Gentile and Jew, just the tacit agreement to remain socially separate.

Jews and Gentiles rarely dated one another. I knew of only two abrogations of this unspoken custom: a boy named Don Neugabauer dated a girl named Diane Fishman and a girl named Joyce Cortina dated a boy named Billy Fish. I suspect neither of these girls' parents was much pleased. In my four years at Senn, I don't believe it ever even occurred to me to ask out a Gentile girl, though I would later go on to marry two non-Jewish women.

Social clubs at Senn were, with rare exceptions, separated by whether their members were Jewish or Gentile. These clubs were crucial to one's social life and established one's social status within the school. Clubs held weekly meetings; boys' clubs competed in softball and touch-football games at Waveland Park off Lake Shore Drive, and held dances, some quite large, at such hotels as the Palmer House and the Edgewater Beach. At one such dance I can recall the Crew Cuts appeared, singing their then recent hit song "Sh-Boom." The Mert Davis Dance, named after a boy who died of polio, collected somewhere in the neighborhood of $20,000 for the fight against the disease.

In the organization of clubs, the Jewish kids were more ambitious than the Gentile. Some Jewish clubs, the Ravens, the Iaetas, the Gargoyles, included members from freshman through senior year, and, imitating college fraternities, required pledging. Others were made up exclusively of kids in the same year (Majestics, Dukes, Olympians, Vagabonds, Imperials). Only two Gentile boys' clubs, Delta and Beta, existed; their members were what we called "hoods": DA hairdos, boxcar loafers, low-slung Levi's identified a hood. Standard duds for non-hoods was a V-neck cashmere sweater worn over a white T-shirt, chino pants or Levi's, loafers. (A small, odd segment of male students wore clothes from a Halsted Street shop off Maxwell Street called Smoky Joe's, which featured pegged pants of rust or electric-blue color with outer seams, Billy Eckstine high-collared shirts, blue suede shoes.) The one club that had both Jews and Gentiles was called Alpha, and its members tended to be athletes who played for the school's various teams. A senior boys honorary club called the Green and White (the school's colors) was sponsored by the school, election to which was supposedly based on one's all-round merit during one's years there. Girls at Senn had their own clubs, with such names as Chiquitas, Gott a Cop (a Guy), Fidels, Debs, and more. In the exchange between classes one witnessed a blaze of the different colors of the various club jackets worn by both girls and boys. If one were going steady with a girl, she sometimes wore your club jacket or letter sweater, the cloth version of an engagement ring.

In the intricacy and elaborateness of its status system, Senn High School during my years there compared with that of the court of the Sun King, though with no Duc de Saint-Simon to describe and explain it. One could tell the status of a kid by the club jacket he or she was wearing. A Raynor was not in the same class as an Olympian, a Noble in that of a Raven. Some kids steered clear entirely of these fraternities and clubs. I was not among them. As a freshman, I pledged and became a member of the Iaetas; having left the Iaetas in my sophomore year, in my junior year I was made an honorary member of the Ravens—"honorary" in that I was not required to pledge—and the same year was invited to join Alpha.

In Latin, *laetas* (with an *l*) means happy, glad, joyous; no meaning for the word "Iaetas" (with an *I*) is available in any language I know. The fraternity may well have been founded on a typo. In any case, the Iaetas were made up of rather adventurous boys of various social classes. Some lived in West Rogers Park (which tended to be Raven country), but more lived in the neighborhood around Argyle Street and Sheridan Road. A few of their families were working-class; others had fathers who were less than successful salesmen and lived in furnished apartments in the Argyle-Sheridan neighborhood.

The epitome Iaeta was Frankie Sommers, a boy two years older than I. Frankie's father worked as a *schneider*, or corned beef and pastrami cutter, at a Sheridan Road delicatessen. Frankie was among the crowd known as the Argyle boys. He was an excellent athlete: a center fielder in softball, a tailback in touch football, on the school's junior (five foot eight and under) basketball team. Small, handsome, he had the muscularity of a gymnast, a good laugh, and an easy temperament. He was also a terrific dancer, jitterbug his specialty. At dances, when he and his girlfriend, Nancy Schaffner, jitterbugged, the floor cleared as in a Fred Astaire or Gene Kelly movie, everyone stepping aside to watch Frankie gracefully twirl and flip Nancy around. Later in life he became a physical therapist and, now married to Nancy, moved to Peoria, Illinois. My best guess is that Frankie Sommers peaked in high school.

I, meanwhile, had somehow or other trained myself to attain to the apotheosis of that day, "the good guy." The good guy was a listener, never pushing himself forward; a boy with a store of interesting anecdotes, many of them self-deprecating. He had a wide tolerance, was someone you could confide in. He was familiar, easy to be with. In those high school years I was known as Eppy, sometimes Ep, a good name for a good guy. "A good guy, Ep, and funny, too."

Like many of the Iaetas, I lunched not in the school cafeteria but at Harry's, a school store and restaurant just outside the school, where I had my first BLT (thirty-five cents). I began and ended my school day at Harry's. A cigarette smoker by my sophomore year, as were most of my friends, my tiffin, or second breakfast before classes began, was a root beer in a mug, a brownie, and a Lucky Strike.

Harry's was the scene of much laughter and limitless bugging. "Bugging" was the word we used for the elaborate and nearly relentless teasing we boys did to one another. Each of us a Don Rickles in training, we specialized in comic put-downs. If anyone among us had an odd physical trait, it was registered by bugging: so a kid named Bob Cole who had a large nose became Jose Noseay; a boy named Dan Brodsky with slanting eyes became the Mikado; a boy named Billy Greengoss who was only slightly overweight became the Swine; Ronny Engel, smaller and younger than Billy, was Junior Swine. The combination of beginning face hair and light acne was known as "tweed," and my friend Loren Singer become Boss Tweed, later just Boss. Because he emitted a barely discernible croaking sound in his deep baritone voice, Phil Kaufman became Froggy. Alan Mitchell, who had a chipped front tooth, became for all his days Jagtooth.

The only class in my four years at Senn that aroused my interest, as noted, was geometry. Well taught by a middle-aged woman named Mrs. Hackman, geometry, with its theorems, axioms, and economically formulated problems satisfied what must have been a hidden ardor for order in me. Solving a geometry problem provided a clean satisfaction that no other schoolwork did. Not that I excelled in the class, but at least I wasn't bored blue by it.

Seated next to me in geometry was a boy two years older than I named Harry Shadian. Harry played on the junior basketball team. He was legendary for supposedly staying up the better part of the night before measuring in at five eight, when he was probably five eleven; he was said to have accomplished this by walking around with a friend named Dick Burkholder on his shoulders, thereby giving him the natural slump that allowed him to pass for five eight at the official measurement. After the second day of class, Harry met me in the hall and told me that he hadn't a chance of passing this course without my help. Could he copy my homework, he asked, and also in class lean over and copy my exams? Of course, I told him. How could I, a good guy, possibly refuse?

During my last two high school years, through the auspices of my father, I worked Saturdays and on holidays at a store at the busy Chicago Loop corner of State and Randolph called Shoppers Corner, which sold clothes, costume jewelry, and other odd items. Two of the men I worked with selling jewelry—free engraving on identification bracelets—were alcoholics, but also nice men. One of my lasting memories of the job is of one Saturday noting a man standing outside the shop looking in, specifically at me. He must have been there no fewer than three hours, and when at the end of my workday I departed the shop, he approached and asked if he could buy me dinner at his hotel. Clearly this was a homosexual hit. I told him that I should normally like to do so, but I was studying to become a priest and so it was quite impossible, but thanked him anyway.

If anyone were caught shoplifting from Shoppers Corner, he was taken down to the basement by one of the two bosses—an Englishman named Hymie Glass or his partner, Jerry Feingold—roughed up a bit, and told that if he ever returned to the store the cops would be called. In the end, all the money he had on him, apart from twenty-five cents for bus or El fare, was taken from him. Women as well as men were often caught shoplifting. I felt a shower of sympathy for them as they were escorted outside the store, sometimes in tears.

Sophomore year at Senn, I fell in with Jeremy Klein (the name has been changed to protect the guilty), roughly two years older than I, who also played junior basketball, though that was the least extraordinary thing about him. Jeremy was small, clear-featured, almost preternaturally clean, seeming at all times as if he had just emerged from a shower. He had an air of seriousness about him; he smiled a fair amount, but rarely laughed. He was smart, which is different from being merely intelligent. In sports he never made a mistake. He was a superior gin rummy player. He could be salesmanly when salesmanship was required, winning, for example, the approval of parents when he needed it. He was also, not entirely through his own fault, immensely corrupt.

As for this corruption, Jeremy came to it through inheritance—specifically, through his father. Lou Klein was what in Chicago was known as a borax man—that is, a home improvements salesman not entirely on the legit. He had acquired the Chicago franchise for a firm selling windows and doors, and now employed a dozen or so borax men of his own. I went with Jeremy one day to his father's office in midafternoon and discovered Lou Klein in what looked like a high-stakes poker game played on a conference table with some of his salesmen. How different, I thought at the time, from my own father, who viewed what he called "his place of business" as a serious if not slightly sacred precinct.

As a boy of sixteen and seventeen, Jeremy walked around with never less than a hundred bucks in his pocket; this in the day when a normal allowance for a high school kid was $5. He had his own car, a current-year green Chevy hardtop convertible. One afternoon he was planning to spend some time with his girlfriend, whose parents weren't at home, but didn't want anyone to see his car parked in front of her house. I told him I could take care of it for him, dropped him off, and drove away, neglecting to tell him that I hadn't a driver's license. During the next two hours, I drove round the quiet neighborhood, teaching myself to drive in Jeremy's Chevy.

Lou Klein later took an interest in boxing and acquired a majority interest in a few boxers. Boxing in those days was Syndicate, or Mob, territory, and at one point Lou Klein—the local press referred to him as Lou ("Hawkface") Klein—was simultaneously being pursued by the FBI and a vicious Syndicate hit man named Felix "Milwaukee Phil" Alderisio. Fortunately, the FBI got to him first. Lou Kein subsequently retired into the job of property manager, and henceforth stayed out of the papers.

What Jeremy saw in me I do not know. But I became, in effect, his protégé. He fixed me up with the younger sister of his girlfriend. He gave me mini-lectures on sex education much more detailed than my father's ("You want to be careful"). The story was told that his father's pals once gave Jeremy $50 to go at it with two lesbian prostitutes while they watched. Jeremy and I hung out together for a year or so. On one occasion, we drove off to a whorehouse in the town of Braidwood, Illinois, which was closed, so we got back into Jeremy's Chevy and drove across state to another whorehouse in Kankakee. At the end of an early evening's card game, Jeremy and I would sometimes go off together to the sulky races in the western suburbs of Maywood. Jeremy was always, as the gambler's say, in action, and life with him was for me never less than exciting.

Late in our friendship, not long before he went off to college, Jeremy suggested I hide behind the bar of his family's finished basement while he had sex with his girlfriend. Why he needed an eyewitness for his bonking, I do not know. I'm pleased to say that I told him I had no interest in doing so, and to this day am glad I didn't, for to have done so, I sensed even then, would have been to demean myself.

Jeremy's and my friendship didn't so much break up as drift away.

He went off to the University of Michigan, after a year or so of which, discovering the place didn't have much to offer him, he dropped out. Jeremy became a bookie, which he remained for the rest of his life. In 2007 he went to *cheder*, as Jewish crooks called prison, for refusing to testify against local Mafia guys—testimony that figured to have put his life in danger—though he wasn't there for long. I always thought, with his brains and charm, Jeremy could have done much better than he did, but being a bookie, I suppose, kept him in action full-time, and perhaps staying perpetually in action was what he needed.

We Jewish boys, at least those in my circle, loosely modeled ourselves on mafiosi, without of course the killing or the crime. (In Chicago, organized crime was never referred to as Mafia, but instead as the Syndicate, the Mob, the Organization, the Boys.) Gambling and whoring, which we did go in for, were, for many of us, along with our notion of a good time, an imitation at a low level of Syndicate life.

Jews were not at the center of the Syndicate, but there were a number of Jews in and around the periphery of the Chicago Syndicate. The Jewish Jake "Greasy Thumb" Guzik served as legal and financial adviser to the Syndicate. A number of Jews were bookies, including Marty Sommerfield's father, Jakie. The son of another Jewish bookie named Potsy Pearl was a good friend of my brother. Phil Levin, the father of a girl named Nancy, whom I dated, seemed never to work. From spring through autumn, he golfed; from autumn until spring he played gin at the Town Club atop the Sheraton Hotel. He was married to a beautiful woman, formerly one of the chorus girls known as the Chez Paree Adorables. I learned that Phil Levin was the brother of a Capone lieutenant named "Loudmouth" Hymie Levin. As part of his brother's legacy,

Phil was rumored to collect a dollar a month on every jukebox in Chicago.

The Syndicate was a palpable presence in Chicago. One of the local television stations assigned a reporter to cover Syndicate doings exclusively. The city's first ward, its downtown, was said to be under Syndicate control. Tony "Big Tuna" Accardo was a name as well known in the city as that of Ernie Banks. One heard stories of Syndicate underlings bullying people on country club golf courses. Syndicate rumors were rife. The father of a friend of mine, who had a successful business supplying sheets and towels to Loop hotels, was said to be Syndicate connected. My father had an Italian customer who one day told him that if he ever needed any extra dough, the Boys would be glad to help out. "Just what I need," my father said, recounting the story, "those monsters as my partners."

Taking our cue from the Syndicate, my friends' and my participation in our low-grade illicit activities gave life an added tang. Most in my circle of high school friends at one time or another availed themselves of the services of prostitutes. (So, too, in their day, it pleases me to report, did Charles Lamb, William Hazlitt, William Wordsworth, and John Keats.) Some might have done so out of sexual heat, but for most of us I don't believe sex was the main motive. The sex, truth to tell, was not much beyond perfunctory. At the bordellos of Braidwood or Kankakee, and later at Danville, the woman you had chosen to be with checked you for venereal disease and then instructed you not to bother taking off your socks, shirt, or sweater. The menu included straight sex for $3, half-and-half (fellatio and fornication) for $5, and something called "around the world" (don't ask) for $10. The money was collected up front. The actual bonking, or sex, didn't take long.

("Wham, bam, thank you, ma'am.") In his autobiography, *Because I Was Flesh*, Edward Dahlberg writes that "prostitutes are as essential to a society as potatoes, bread, and meat, though they may not be rhapsodical food." Of his own first visit to a prostitute in Kansas City, Dahlberg writes: "My experience with this woman was very brief, and of no value to her. It is told that twilight in Quito lasts no longer than three minutes—which was longer than my intimacy with her." And afterward: "I hurried into my trousers and shirt as if I were getting into my morals."

Going to whorehouses in the Chicago of my youth was a boyhood ritual, as much amusing adventure as a necessary release of sexual energy. The sixty-or-so-mile ride to Braidwood or Kankakee featured much joking, especially if a novice were along. ("Remember, Danny, whatever you do, don't let her get her legs outside yours.") On the way back, just past the Wacker Street Bridge on Chicago's Outer Drive, there was in those days a sign for Dad's Old Fashioned Root Beer that read "Have You Had It Lately?" which was always good for a rousing laugh.

My own whoremongering was restricted to perhaps a dozen times. One notable place—4221 South St. Lawrence, the address sticks in my mind after all these years—was the apartment of Iona Satterfield, wife (some said sister) of the glass-jawed heavyweight boxer Bob Satterfield. That four Jewish boys could go into this all-Black neighborhood, park the red-and-white Buick Roadmaster of Larry Goldenberg's father, and walk up to the second floor of a building that still had mezuzahs on many of its doorjambs from earlier tenants, without interference or the least nervousness, shows the wild difference between that day (1953) and this.

Iona was biracial, and strikingly elegant. Years later I saw her driving down Stony Island Avenue in a maroon Lincoln convertible with its top down. She was the madam and had three or four girls working for her. After my brief bout with one of them, I used the bathroom in the apartment, atop whose tank I noted a dish with a burnt spoon resting upon it, which went a long way toward explaining why some young women might have turned to prostitution.

Prostitution moderately flourished until sometime in the 1960s, when nice girls, giving it away for nothing, largely put it out of business. A nice girl in the 1950s did not, could not, risk sleeping with a boy. Through high school I had two extended relationships, both entailing what in that day was known as "heavy petting"; but what was known as "going all the way" was unthinkable. Not even I, as salacious as any adolescent, thought going all the way a real possibility.

That is, until one summer day, at Farewell Beach, I met Larry Lauer, a friend from Sheridan Road days whom I hadn't seen for years. His family had since come up in the world and moved to the suburb of Wilmette. He was off to college in the fall. We talked for a bit about the old days, then he asked me if I had any interest in the phone number of a nymphomaniac of his acquaintance. "Of course," I said, and he wrote down the name of a girl a year or so younger than I whom I shall call Letitia Rogers.

I called Letitia a day or two later to set up a date. She was a smallish girl, pretty, even a touch shy, who went to nearby Sullivan High School. We went that night to a drive-in movie, and in the back seat of my mother's then car, a Chevy Bel Air, did the much-yearned-for and seldom-done deed. We did it on three or four other occasions: again at the drive-in, once by the Skokie Lagoons, and I don't remember where else. In an act I am even now ashamed of, I told my friends about my good luck. I even told a civics teacher at Senn, a man then in his late twenties with whom I enjoyed a special relationship, mentioning that I wished I could find a better place to be with Letitia. He suggested I bring her to his apartment, which I did. After my brief roll with Letitia, he took my place with her on his couch. I never returned to his apartment.

As for Letitia's supposed "nymphomania," it didn't of course really exist. Nymphomania, I have come to believe, is a male fantasy, the fantasy that holds that all women ardently want sex and can never get enough of it. I never came to know Letitia all that well, but my best guess is that she was a sadly neurotic girl who was fearful of saying no to boys. The reason I never came to know Letitia well is that one day I came home to learn that her parents had called mine to report that I had been saying terrible things about their daughter, and they wanted it stopped, now, or they would report me to my school principal, if not to the police. My father, in recounting this phone call, made plain his disappointment in me. Only years later did I become disappointed in myself for such behavior.

Mine was a full high school life, all of it lived outside the classroom. I dated, I played on the frosh-soph basketball team, I lettered in tennis, but gambling, chiefly playing cards, dominated all else in my life. Football parlay cards, on which you picked three college football games with the appropriate point spreads for a six-to-one payoff, were available at a couple of newsstands in West Rogers Park and also handed out by a few enterprising students at Senn. Card games, gin rummy (Hollywood-Oklahoma, spades double), but chiefly poker (five-card draw, seven-card stud, high-low, deuces sometimes wild, more often not), we played at one another's homes, after school, on holidays, and on weekend nights. The stakes at first were moderate: gin games were played for a tenth-, sometimes a fifth-of-a-cent a point; poker games usually entailed nickel, dime, and quarter bets.

Then some unknown genius invented a game called potluck. In potluck, the dealer put a sum in the middle of the table, and played blackjack, one hand at a time, with players betting any part of the pot they wished, while the dealer was unable to take his money out until it amounted to three times what he had initially put in the pot. An automatic escalating element was entailed. As the game wore on and one was down, say, $20, one was likely to put $10 or $20 in the pot, needing $30 or $60 to pull one's money out. Meanwhile, if dealt an ace, there was always the temptation for players not dealing to call out, "Pot it," which meant one was betting everything in the pot. Suddenly, there were $50, $60, or $90 winners or losers at the end of potluck games.

I once lost seventy-odd bucks between after school and before dinner, a dinner that did not taste all that good on that particular night. I recall a memorable all-night potluck game at the 3800 North Lake Shore Drive apartment of Dickie "The Owl" Levinson, whose parents were out of town. I remember an afternoon game at the home of Jimmy Fox in which two players—Ronny Harris and Michael Gurvey—having lost all their money, departed to shovel snow, returned ninety minutes or so later, and in one bet lost the $10 they had made shoveling. On our senior trip to Washington, I never left the train to visit the Capitol, the Supreme Court, and other national buildings and monuments, but remained aboard with friends playing cards.

The semester before my high school days ended, I was elected to the Green and White, the boys' senior honorary society. One morning, two of its members came to my homeroom to inform me of the honor. I told them thanks anyway, but I would pass, claiming I had too many other things going on in my life. Apparently no one before had ever turned down the Green and White. I was the talk of Harry's that afternoon. The word wasn't yet in currency, but by turning down membership in the Green and White I had my first taste of the pleasure of being anti-establishment. Could one be both a conformist and anti-establishment? Apparently one could, for that is what I was as a high school boy. In a world that has never known a shortage of contradictions, who says one can't have it both ways?

My one regret from my high school days is that I didn't somehow let my homeroom teacher, Miss (never Ms.) Edna Burke, know how much I came to admire her. A music teacher, tall, well into middle age, often wearing a gray gabardine suit, a spinster, there was a kindness and grandeur about her that I only came to recognize in my last year in high school. I shall always remember her, seated at the piano, playing with many an arpeggio and singing in high soprano—"They asked me how I knew my true love was true"—"Smoke Gets in Your Eyes." No matter how miscreant the behavior of students, she kept her calm, her dignity, her cool. Dear Miss Burke, I hope your last years were gentle and pleasing ones.

Each morning during my high school years I woke with nothing but pleasant prospects awaiting. Gambling, whoring, bugging, smoking, laughing—lots of laughing—freedom from responsibility, high school was paradise.

Chapter Five

Joe College

"If you want to go to college," my father said, "the money's there and I'll pay for it. But I wonder if you wouldn't be wasting your time. I personally think you'd make an excellent salesman." A compliment was implied here, for my father, without college, without even finishing high school, was himself an excellent, and successful, salesman. Yet I never doubted I would go to college, not because I was eager for knowledge, or had anything special in mind in doing so, but chiefly because I wasn't ready to go to work in a serious way, and, good conformist that I was, I wanted to go because all my friends were going.

As for which college, the choice was never in doubt. The University of Illinois at Champaign-Urbana was the only possibility. In those days, if you lived in the state, University of Illinois had, in effect, open enrollment. My memory is that the tuition for in-state residents was $90 a semester.

As for what I would study, I hadn't a clue. Most of my friends, to establish their seriousness, became business majors. The prospect of doing likewise was for me not only dreary but a touch daunting. Studying accounting, for example, was unthinkable. ("Lloydie, don't be a schmuck," a friend of mine's father replied when he told him he was interested in studying accounting. "You don't study accounting. You hire an accountant.") That left something called liberal arts, a term until then I had never heard. Liberal arts meant taking a foreign language, literature, history, philosophy, soft stuff. *What the hell, why not*, I thought. *Better than the dry bones of business.* When philistine members of my extended family asked me what I was studying, rather than say literature, philosophy, or history, I would say "pre-law," which put an end to their questioning.

The other decision I had to make, which was really no decision at all, was whether or not to join a fraternity. Of course I would join a fraternity. My senior year in high school, fraternity guys from Illinois had already begun, as the phrase was, to rush me. During my teaching days at Northwestern University, I had a student named Pano Kanelos, the son of a Greek immigrant, and himself later the president of St. John's College and the founding president of the University of Austin. When Pano was in his senior year in high school and deciding what college to attend, his father instructed him seriously to consider going to Ohio State University. When Pano asked why Ohio State, his father said: "Because I look at the catalogue, Pano, and see that Ohio State University is sixty percent Greek." I don't know what percentage of the University of Illinois was Greek in 1955, but what was well known was that, in a large and otherwise rather impersonal campus, joining a fraternity supplied one with better food, a ready-made social life, and a sense of belonging.

Fraternities at Illinois, and just about everywhere else, were strictly segregated between Gentiles and Jews. No one in those days saw any reason for complaint about this arrangement. At the time at Illinois, there were seven Jewish fraternities and four Jewish sororities. Of the fraternities, each had its own character, its own cachet. During rush week, I stayed at the Phi Epsilon Pi house, which more than suggested I would end up pledging that fraternity, which I eventually did. Phi Ep stood for a certain seriousness; many among its members were studying to be physicians, engineers, architects. The accumulated grade point average of its members was high; it did well in interfraternity sports; and scored well in Stunt Show, an event in which a fraternity joined with a sorority to put on a Broadway-like song-and-dance number.

And yet I had my doubts. Jack Libby, my old friend from Sheridan Road days, asked me to spend at least one day at Tau Epsilon Phi, his fraternity. Jack's spirit of adventurous good humor was always appealing to me. At Phi Ep, they said a benediction before dinner. At the dinner I attended at the TEP house, the president of the fraternity asked Jack to say the benediction. "Lordy, Lordy, Lordy," he said, "let's all sit down and eat." Which nicely summed up the difference between the Phi Eps and the TEPs: earnestness as opposed to jollity.

Jack was majoring in business, but was said to ask members of his fraternity to hide his books until the month of November, when he would begin studying in earnest. Women found Jack, with his dark good looks, attractive. He was a gambler. In later days, after I had become a member of Phi Ep, he suggested we go in as partners in betting among our respective fraternity brothers against Illinois in an important Illinois-Iowa basketball game. His plan was to give a false point spread, then take the money—some $400 raised between us—and lay it off on his bookie in Urbana, hoping that we could fall between our false and the real point spread, thus collecting $800. Iowa won, but the plan didn't work out. We didn't make our point spread, and Jack and I broke even, though everyone thought we had won. At the TEP house, they threw Jack in the shower.

For some reason Jack continued to look out for me. He fixed me up at Illinois with a "fast" girl. In later years he did so again with a woman who lived in Prairie Shores, one of the first integrated high-rise housing units in Chicago. We lost touch when Jack moved to Memphis, where he married a woman whose family was said to own one of the largest furniture stores in the city. Jack took a pass on going into the business, and instead started a borax operation selling home improvements out of a basement boiler room. He, too, more likely than not, couldn't do without the action. Once, when I was working for the anti-poverty program in Little Rock, my plane to Chicago made a stop in Memphis and I phoned Jack. When he asked me what I was doing, I said I was working for the government. "I am, too," he replied. "It has a hundred-thousand-dollar lien on my business."

As for a fraternity, in the end, as I said, I chose Phi Ep, the safer choice. I knew a few likable fellows from Senn High School who were members, and I was impressed by its emphasis on academic achievement—grade point average and all that—for I was myself more than a touch worried about making grades. I was driven to the Twelfth Street railroad station to go off to the University of Illinois by my friend Loren Singer, who specialized in unwanted frank opinions, and who, dropping me off, said, "I'll see you in six months after you flunk out." *Please, God, prove him wrong,* I thought at the time. Genial screw-off though I thought myself, I urgently wanted to avoid the humiliation of flunking out of college.

At Phi Ep, pledges were required during the week to sit in the house dining room from 7:30 to 10:00 p.m. for study. I found this less a torture than I had supposed. I was more than a little pleased to discover that I had the *sitzfleisch*, or bottom patience, to do so. As for my courses—French, rhetoric (the name for basic composition), biology, and poetry, along with physical education and Air Force ROTC (the latter two required in a land-grant school)—none, if I put in the time on them, were especially troubling. I learned, for one thing, that I could write with a modest clarity, though I still found any but the most rudimentary punctuation worrisome and steered clear of any use of semicolons, dashes, or parentheses.

My French course was taught by a man named Philip Kolb, whom in my Middle Western naïveté I was certain was himself French, but who turned out to be born in Chicago. He was the editor of the French edition of the fifty-odd-volume correspondence of Marcel Proust. Why a man devoted to so elevated a task had to teach the rudiments of French to freshman students, I do not know. I do know he was an excellent teacher. In that French course the fellow sitting next to me, Fred McNally by name, asked if he could copy any quizzes or exams off me. I agreed to his doing so. (Shades of Harry Shadian.) Throughout the semester, when called upon, McNally invariably answered, "Beats me." Poetry, a survey course of sorts, offered no great problems. I finished my first semester with just above a B average.

That summer, hoping to widen my intellectual horizon, I took a course in the novel at the University of Illinois in Chicago, then located at Navy Pier. The school in those days was known as Harvard on the Rocks. The course was taught by a man with a *mittel*-European accent, and included novels by Flaubert, Stendhal, Balzac, George Eliot, and others. Often, he would ask us what some passage or character or scene reminded us of. The answers might be, in his accented English, "Ze Rape of ze Lock," "Ze beginning of ze *Aeneid*," "Ze famous passage in T. S. Eliot's *Ze Vastelund*." Nothing, of course, ever reminded me or my fellow students of anything. "Vat do you do viz your time?" he once exasperatingly asked. This class was my first encounter with my own want of culture, and I didn't feel at all good about it.

In Champaign, the Phi Ep fraternity occupied my time quite as much as the classroom. In good part, Phi Ep's status derived from the social background of its membership, or rather from that of a handful of its members. The collective identity of some fraternities might be based on a single member, usually an athlete. Around this time, for example, Sigma Chi seemed to be totally epitomized in the person of one Hiles Stout, a football and baseball player from Peoria. Stout *was* Sigma Chi: small-town, blond crew cut, burly, not likely to have been among the six hundred subscribers to T. S. Eliot's the *Criterion*.

Phi Ep was not so conveniently summed up in one person. But the typical member would have come from the Chicago area, probably either from one of the more prosperous Jewish suburbs to the north or from Lake Shore Drive. He would be slender, well-turned-out—his principal source of haberdashery Brooks Brothers—and with hair worn short and parted to one side, in the style then known as the

"Princeton." While his father probably made his money working for someone else, or had a small business of his own, he himself would be headed for the professions—medicine, law, dentistry, accountancy, possibly engineering. There would be a self-assurance about him, a studied casualness that came from a sense of being at ease in the world. And the truth is, he really was at ease in the world; he knew where he wanted to go and and had a pretty good idea of how to get there.

Twelve of us were in the Phi Ep pledge class that year and for the most part we were a fairly similar lot; or at any rate, most of us dressed and talked roughly alike and seemed to share roughly similar values. Most, but not all of us. The twelfth member of the pledge class, Marvin Schmidt I shall call him, was another story. Not to put too fine a point on it, his clothes were wrong, his style was wrong, he really didn't quite fit in. Schmidt was an engineering student, and the sole reason he was asked to pledge Phi Ep was that one of the members, an upperclassman from a small town in Arkansas who also studied engineering, wanted an engineer for the pledge class and was able to prevail. But Schmidt excepted, we were the pick of the pack, the best there was, the most intensely sought-after candidates for the Jewish fraternities to come downstate in February of 1955, and there was, I suppose, a certain pride in that.

Once settled in, pledging was not as irksome as I feared it might be. Unlike most of the other fraternities on campus, the Phi Eps did not paddle their pledges—a sign of their superior civility. One pledge was assigned to each table in the dining room and we were all instructed in a rigid set of table manners: knife placed across upper-right portion of plate, blade turned in; all food both passed and received across the body; and so forth. Each morning two of us were assigned wake-up call, which involved waking the members—gently, oh, ever so gently—for their morning classes. After lunch and often after classes we ran errands: picking up members' laundry or dropping it off, fetching a book from the library, buying a packet of envelopes, or picking up clothes from the dry cleaner's. Saturday mornings we did a general housecleaning.

Pledges slept in a common dormitory on the top floor of the fraternity house. Each of us was also assigned to a member's room, where we kept our clothes and books. I drew Sam Sax as my roommate. Sammy was the son of a multimillionaire, a self-made man who owned, along with other holdings, the Exchange National Bank in Chicago and the Saxony Hotel, then the premier hotel in Miami Beach. "I'm glad you're going to be my roommate," Sammy said when I arrived at his room with my books and suitcase. "I was worried I'd get that German kid, Schmitz, or whatever his name is." Sammy proved an amiable roommate, being, as it turned out, rarely there. A graduating senior, engaged and soon to be married, he seemed to spend most of his time aloft in airplanes, carrying out obscure, though clearly not petty, errands for his father's various businesses. Within less than ten years, he would be president of his father's bank in Chicago. From photographs that appeared from time to time in the Chicago press, he seemed not to age at all—at thirty-five, as at twenty-one, he still looked fifty-four. Short, pudgy, already nearly bald in his last year at college, it was as if the fates, in endowing Sammy so well financially, had exacted his youth in exchange.

But then, nearly all the seniors among the Phi Eps seemed almost excessively mature. A kind of heavy seriousness, thick with sobriety, was the model not merely aspired to but generally achieved. The Phi Ep seniors *were* older men, and though only just past adolescence, touched with the gift—curse?—of perpetual early middle age. Hal Goodman, the president of Phi Ep at that time, had all the playfulness of a member of the president's Council of Economic Advisers. Dark and extremely earnest, he wore the same sweaters and chino pants that everyone else did during the week, but never seemed quite convincing in them. It was only in a suit, and at that rather a severe business suit, that he looked at home and really comfortable.

Once I began living at the fraternity, it began to take on a different, more variegated, less idealized look. A common fraternity phenomenon in those days was the "closet case," a member who had either been left as a legacy from some Phi Ep older brother or who simply represented a mistake in judgment, a lapse of discrimination, during rush week. These unfortunates were asked not to show up at certain important occasions—rush weeks, big dances, exchanges with desirable sororities. Phi Ep had no formal closet cases, though it did have a number of members whom it chose, so to say, not to feature too prominently. These ranged from Bernie "The Animal" Lefkovitz to Kent Perlberg. I liked the Animal from the start: hairy, rough, he was what he was, with no airs about him. Kent was something else again—a fop of such extraordinary dimension, a character so clearly made of cardboard, that he would be unbelievable in the pages of a novel. Soon after I had unpacked my things in Sammy Sax's room, Kent came by to inspect my ties, which hung on a rack against the door. "Not bad at all," he commented with gravity. "You should see Schmidt's." And here he made a face—a wrinkling of the nose, a puckering of the mouth—appropriate only after the swallowing of some small vile animal. My own foulards, challis, reps, I should gauge, rated from him somewhere between a C+ and a B–.

Phi Ep also had a number of members who did not come from Chicago and were known as the "out-of-towners." At most they comprised perhaps 15 percent of the membership—and in general they tended to fall a cut below the Phi Eps who came from Chicago. They were from such places as Paragould (Arkansas), Minneapolis, Memphis, Sioux City (Iowa); from as far away as New York City and from as nearby as the Illinois towns of Springfield, Mattoon, and Peoria. The out-of-towners were thought of as having made the fraternity seem somehow less parochial. Since no one knew very much about them, most arrived with rather impressive pasts. The member from Paragould, for example, was said to have been an All-State football player in Arkansas. The one from New York—he was in the pledge class preceding mine—claimed to have been offered a bonus to pitch for a major-league baseball team, as well as to have scored higher than anyone else in the history of certain Regents exams. He was a fibber of such magnitude, such purity, such transparency, that one would have had to strain to dislike him. A pre-med, he took great pains never to be caught studying, but would announce the highest grades on exams nonetheless. He would return from the simplest coffee date or movie with his face strewn with lipstick, quite possibly self-applied.

For our pledge-class dance, we did an elaborate revue called *New Faces of 58.50*—*58* for the year and the *.50* for the new February pledge class—which we worked on for about six weeks, honing our thin parodies of the original *New Faces of 1952* show tunes into bland perfection. But this was nothing compared to the fraternity's effort for Stunt Show. The competition did not take place until late in the fall, but rehearsals started the previous summer. Once the school year began, those Phi Eps involved in the show would troop over to our sorority partners every night for further rehearsals. As the competition drew closer, weekends, too, were taken up with rehearsals. No matter which sorority was involved, Phi Ep invariably made the finals.

More was felt to be at stake than the Stunt Show competition itself. The hope was to win the thing so that the following year Phi Ep could have as its partner one of the great Wright Street sorority houses. Wright Street faced the main campus, and lining it were the sororities of Kappa Alpha Theta, Pi Beta Phi, and Kappa Kappa Gamma, none of them Jewish. In those years America still seemed a country of small towns and much under Protestant domination. The plan at Phi Ep, though it was never worked out in a dank basement on a pool table under a bare light bulb, was to sing and dance its way into the heart of America, or—what was much the same thing—into the living room of the Theta house.

Here was another example of the ambiguous—also ambivalent—Jewish attitude toward the Gentile world. On the one hand, Jews felt themselves excluded from this world; on the other, they were mildly contemptuous of it. A Pi Phi might well be beautiful, but she also figured to be, how should one say, more than a touch unimaginative; a girl to take out on dates, but decidedly not to marry.

In case I make myself sound superior to all this, I should emphasize that I was as good and obedient a pledge as any of my brothers and, at least initially, accepted the views prevalent in the fraternity. Like every other pledge, I did as I was told and meekly submitted to the humiliations to which a pledge was subjected.

One such humiliation that stands out is the time we pledges were awakened late at night and marched down from our dormitory to the living room by Al Samuels, the Paragouldian, known for his appetite for coarse humor. We expected the worst. The worst, which we had all heard about, was something called, with brutal simplicity, "The Meat," a very rude exercise having to do with getting a raw piece of steak up and down a staircase while naked and without the use of one's hands or mouth. It was a stunt calculated to bring about solidarity throughout the pledge class by humiliating each of us in precise equal measure.

After lining us up in the living room, Samuels, with a great show of false anger, began with verbal abuse. We were a terrible pledge class, he shrieked, one of the worst ever to come through the house, and he, for one, was goddamn sick of us. We would shape the hell up, fast, or answer to him. He walked down the line, blasting each of us in turn. Then he put us through calisthenics: push-ups, sit-ups, deep knee bends. Next we were told to strip. We all did so, except for Billy Schoenwald. The son of the Chicago fight promoter Irv Schoenwald, Billy, though small, was a tough kid; normally even-tempered, he had a notably low tolerance for taking insults. As the rest of us stood there, vulnerable in our nakedness, Billy announced that he didn't care what happened, he wasn't about to take off his pajamas. Samuels went red in the face. He said he was going to leave the room for ten minutes, during which time the rest of us had better convince our pledge brother to strip. If we failed to do so, he could promise us that our lives in Phi Ep would be made more miserable than any of us would care to contemplate. Ten minutes later he returned to find us, Billy included, unanimously naked.

Part of being in Phi Ep, or for that matter in any fraternity, involved going along with the game—and this included members as well as pledges. Ronald Rothenstein, an upperclassman, was large and lumbering. He was the son of a man who had extensive holdings in real estate in Chicago. He seemed temperamentally tired. Yet even Rothenstein, surely the least romantic of figures, when he became pinned—and to become "pinned" in those days meant one was "engaged to be engaged"—went through the traditional pinning serenade like everyone else in the fraternity. Standing in front of the Alpha Epsilon Phi sorority house across the street from Phi Ep, Rothenstein stepped out before the rest of us, and in a voice more appropriate to the reading of a personal bankruptcy statement, sang about how the Rockies may crumble, Gibraltar may tumble, but his love, yes his love, was here to stay.

As the semester wore on toward finals week, one night we pledges were called into the regular Monday night fraternity meeting for a bull session in which each of us was told, singly, of our inadequacies, of how disappointingly we had turned out, of how far short we had fallen of the Phi Ep measure. The week before finals we went through our last ordained ritual of this period, singling out the member who had been hardest on us as pledges throughout the semester. One evening before dinner we grabbed our man, dragged him out behind the house, tied him up, and dumped pancake syrup, sand, and feathers on him as the rest of the Phi Eps looked on. Then came the week of final exams, after which we all, members and pledges, left the campus for the summer.

The fall rush at the start of the following semester was, of course, much more hectic than the winter one had been, and the traffic of potential pledges coming through Phi Ep was thick. The fraternity pretty much knew which incoming freshmen it wanted from Chicago, though it was still sitting in judgment on certain marginal types and kept on the lookout for out-of-town freshmen that no one had any clear line on. The rushees came in regular sessions: some remarkably confident and poised, others nervous in their eagerness to please. They were met by the Phi Eps in the foyer of the house, walked into the living room, shown through the upstairs floors. But all the while, it was they, not Phi Ep, who were on display.

The evenings of rush week were devoted to blackballing sessions—or "spot" meetings, as they were called, for the word "blackball" was never used. At these meetings it was decided who would be offered a bid to pledge and who would not. The meetings ran well into the night, sometimes breaking up at three or four in the morning. As might be imagined, some very fancy talk was entailed, with everyone putting the finest possible point on everything he said. "I don't wish to reiterate what Mickey Schwartz just finished saying," a representative comment might run, "but it seems to me this kid is, on balance, hardly Phi Ep material." Which was, of course, just another way of saying what was apparent to all, but could not be said straight-out: that a rushee was too ugly, too garishly dressed, too aggressive, too shy, too broken-out, too "Jewish," or too something else that put him beyond the Phi Ep pale. Kids were rejected for much the same reasons that I and almost everyone else who sat in on these meetings had rejected the other fraternities on campus to pledge Phi Ep. There was very little subtlety about the procedure—one either approximated the Phi Ep mold or fell irretrievably short of it.

That rush week presented only one noteworthy incident, which involved the blackballing of a "legacy." This particular candidate wasn't, strictly speaking, in that category—technically, to be a legacy either one's father or older brother (or brothers) had to have been a member of the fraternity. This kid's brother-in-law was a Phi Ep who had graduated about three years before and some of the upperclassmen present at the meeting had known him. One of them telephoned the brother-in-law in Chicago, then returned to announce that he would be driving down that night—such was the urgency of the matter—to talk on behalf of the blackballed kid, his wife's younger brother. The major claim against the candidate seemed to be an insufficiency of distinctly admirable qualities. The opposition would take the floor and ceaselessly reiterate, "I don't wish to reiterate, but this kid doesn't show me anything."

Finally, sometime around two in the morning, the brother-in-law arrived. Dark, with a close-cropped haircut, and wearing a light blue cashmere sweater over a white button-down collar shirt, he was still vintage Phi Ep. After being introduced to the meeting at large, he spoke of his young brother-in-law's eagerness to be a Phi Ep. If he were not asked to pledge the fraternity, he said, he very probably would not remain at Illinois for more than a semester. He had chosen to come to school here precisely because of Phi Ep. He was exactly the sort of kid that Phi Ep could make a man of, which after all was one of the things the fraternity was about. Everything, in short, was brought up but the main point: the kid would be unthinkable if he were not a legacy; but, goddamn it, he *was* a legacy, or the closest thing to it! At the next vote, taken while his brother-in-law was out of the room, it was decided that the bid would be extended after all. Tradition had held, and we all shuffled off to bed.

A few weeks after the pledge class of '59 had been assembled and school had gotten underway, my own pledge class was awakened late one night and told that we were on "hell week." During the seven days that followed we got almost no sleep, were made to wear a suit and tie to class, and were allowed out of our suits only to get into work clothes suitable for executing our hell-week project: building a restraining wall roughly three feet high and seventy or so feet long behind the fraternity house. When we were not in class or working on the wall, we were locked into various rooms, sometimes separately, sometimes together, where we were left to study a small, maroon leather-bound book containing the history of Phi Epsilon Pi. At odd hours throughout the week, we were arbitrarily shifted about from room to room; we were shouted at, rather than talked to; members who had been friendly now froze us out. The week droned on, dreary and wearying.

Early Sunday morning, at the end of the week, our initiation was at hand. Phi Ep's ceremony was not, as I have since learned, as elaborate as that of other fraternities, or especially of some sororities, where incoming members were said to have been moved by the ritual to the point of tears. At Phi Ep we were brought down to the living room one by one, blindfolded. When the blindfolds were removed, we found ourselves in a candlelit room with all the curtains drawn. There, as each of my pledge brothers would do, and as every member in that room had done before me, I was put through the litany of Phi Ep's history. I was asked to name its founding members, to recite its historic dates and events, to reel off the names of its various chapters round the country. At the end of it I was told that I had done execrably, and then instructed to enter the chapter room, a small room off the main one that generally served as the site of all-night bridge games. Before this moment it had been exclusively off-limits to pledges.

In this privileged sanctuary the officers of the fraternity awaited me. They asked if I thought I deserved to be initiated into Phi Ep. I mumbled that I did indeed. They asked what I thought I could contribute to the fraternity. I mumbled some clichés about continuing its tradition, augmenting its prestige on campus, and so on. Everyone in the small room then rose to shake my hand. All that remained was to instruct me in the Phi Ep handshake, in the use and meaning of the password, and finally to place the fraternity's pin on my shirt. Again handshakes all around. As I left the chapter room to return to the living room, I was met by applause and still more handshaking.

At lunch that day, after our entire class had been initiated, there was much singing and an air of high self-congratulation. The whole bizarre business had worked, another successful rite of passage had been brought off. Exhausted, I went to bed shortly after lunch, to sleep for seventeen straight hours. Before falling off, I confidently felt that I had arrived.

I evidently suffer from the Groucho Marx syndrome. In a now famous letter of resignation to the Friars Club, Groucho wrote: "I don't want to belong to any club that would accept me as one of its members." I had only to be initiated in Phi Ep, then I lost all interest in it. After a single semester as a member I moved out of the fraternity house to take an apartment with a newly made friend named Ted Laertes, though I continued to take my evening meals at Phi Ep.

I was also beginning to find the University of Illinois tiresome. The school seemed so large, so impersonal. One attended lectures for courses with as many as three or four hundred fellow students in the audience. Outside fraternities and sororities there appeared to be no social life whatsoever. Around this time, in an act of intellectual aspiration, I applied to the University of Chicago, about which I knew very little and about my chances of getting in even less. Nonetheless it seemed worth a shot.

This was just before my being kicked out of the University of Illinois.

Chapter Six

Where Fun Went to Die

I was fairly secure in my ability to take and pass courses at the University of Illinois. The old high school Eppy, though, was still extant. At one point, seated in a large lecture hall, he took a writing exam for a pre-med Phi Ep who feared not passing such an exam. He was still a guy who liked to be in action, as the old gamblers called it, playing in poker games organized by Jack Libby, betting on ball games, stimulated by the illicit.

Which explains why Jon Isenberg, a Phi Ep pledge brother, a business major, came to me to report that, while in the Accounting Department office the day before, he noted and lifted an upcoming Accounting 101 exam and wondered if any use might be made of it. The answer, obviously, was to sell it to students taking Accounting 101. I put myself in charge of the project, with Ted Laertes as my partner.

We made several copies of the stolen exam, and then one night called each of the fraternities on campus to ask how many of their members were taking Accounting 101. Once we learned this, we told the person on the phone that we would sell the exam for $5 for every guy taking the course, and arranged to meet them and deliver the exam. I thought we might be able to clear six or seven hundred dollars on the deal. The first six or seven pickups went well, but on the eighth, an older student (from which fraternity I do not now recall) told us we were, in effect, under arrest for peddling a stolen examination, took our names, and notified us that we would soon be called up before a board of the student government. Somehow they had got Jon Isenberg's name, and those of others who were also selling the accounting exam.

When Ted and I came up before the student government board, all we could plead was remorse. Not good enough, for the young tend to be morally more merciless than the more mature, and we were soon after informed that we were kicked out of the university, as, we later learned, were Jon and the others. The story got into the Chicago press, with our names mentioned.

(Such is the deviousness of that old trickster who goes by the name of Fate, for Jon Isenberg getting kicked out of school turned out to be of the greatest positive significance. He went from being a business student to a pre-med, eventually becoming an internationally known gastroenterologist who, before he died at the age of sixty-six, published 180 papers and was the ninety-fifth president of the American Gastroenterological Association. Had he not stolen the exam and subsequently been kicked out of school he might have ended his days as an accountant.)

When I returned home to Chicago, my father, his disappointment in me once again evident, told me he expected me to find a job as soon as possible. I found one, in the local want ads, the very next day, a few miles from our apartment, working in the receiving department of a company called Fidelitone that manufactured phonograph needles. Perhaps two hundred people worked at Fidelitone, most of them women. Wages were paid on an hourly basis. One clocked in and out with one's card. Everyone ate in the company cafeteria. Some of the workers organized themselves into bowling leagues. To insinuate myself into the factory atmosphere, I claimed that I had been a pre-medical student, but had to drop out, at least for a while, for a want of money. One of the janitors at Fidelitone, an amusing Italian fellow who, with his cousin, snuck off from time to time to take naps behind packing cases, earnestly offered to provide me with dead cats for dissection, thinking that this might be useful to a future medical student.

In the receiving room, I worked for a man in his mid-fifties named Steve Tomz. I remember little about him apart from that he always treated me kindly and the violence of his occasional swearing, which usually had to do with the ripping, tearing, or pulling off of genitals, male and female. I had hoped that the better part of my day would be loading and unloading trucks, which would build up my muscles as a construction job might. But most of it had to do with filling packets of phonograph needles while awaiting the two or three trucks that did arrive daily and needed to be loaded or unloaded. The days, the four months or so of them while I was at Fidelitone, passed quickly enough.

Most nights I spent in the company of Ted Laertes. He had been working for Royal Lumber, his father's home improvements company, spending a good part of them photographing curbs where garages were to be built. Ted in those days had a dark, amusingly oblique sense of humor. He called a pledge brother of mine "Pro," and when I asked him why he did so, he replied that it stands for "'Protozoan,' the world's simplest known animal." We went for drinks, to movies, laughed a lot (in the best gallows humor manner), and shared our worries about our futures, most immediately where we might end up in school in the autumn. Ted eventually returned to the University of Illinois and went on to become a successful money manager.

I, without great hope, was awaiting word from the University of Chicago, to which I had applied before being kicked out of Illinois. I'm not entirely sure why I applied to the University of Chicago. Even though I had lived in the city of Chicago all my life, I had never seen the place. In those days of the House Committee on Un-American Activities, the school was thought radical, even "pinko," or quasi communist. At that time, too, it was better known for its graduate and professional schools than for its undergraduate division; there were roughly six thousand professional and graduate students at the university to two thousand undergraduates. Apart from the older sister of a good friend, I knew no one who had gone there.

The University of Chicago had the reputation of high intellectuality. Great scientific discoveries had been made there, notable among them the splitting of the atom. The university's law school, unlike most other law schools, was said to have been theoretical, more interested in the philosophical aspects of the law than in its applications. The university's economics department, under Frank Knight and Milton Friedman, was coming into its fame. Without a football team, which had been banished by Robert Hutchins when president of the school—"Football has the same relation to education," he said, "that bullfighting has to agriculture"—and having only a handful of fraternities and no sororities, it appealed to the nineteen-year-old kid, me, who had vague intellectual aspirations if little intellectual experience.

By the month of May, still working at Fidelitone, I had not heard from the University of Chicago, and so decided to travel down to Hyde Park to learn of the fate of my application. Straight off I was impressed by the (however false) Gothic architecture of the place. The University of Illinois campus was spread out, and one might have a class a mile or so away from one's previous class. The University of Chicago was set up as a quadrangle, with only its law school on the other side of the Midway Plaisance, the strip of land that was the scene of the 1893 World's Columbian Exposition. I thought the setting grand.

At the administration building, after inquiring about the state of my application to the university, I was sent along to the office of Robert Strozier, the dean of students. A middle-aged man, fully suited and wearing a necktie, as was the custom of the day—I myself wore a sport jacket and necktie for the meeting—he greeted me cordially. I told him I was trying to make plans for the autumn and asked him if he could give me any word about my application to the university. He inquired about how I spelled my name, rose, walked over to a file cabinet, extracted a folder that he quickly glimpsed at, and said: "Yes, sure, you're accepted." He couldn't have known it, and neither could I, but that single sentence—"Yes, sure, you're accepted"—would change my life.

Eager to get back into the harness of college life, I took a course at the University of Chicago that summer. The course was in mathematics and was part of the school's core curriculum. I had planned to live on campus, but for that summer at least I continued to live at home. After the first three-hour morning math class I attended, I discovered that the fellow sitting beside me also lived on the city's North Side. I asked if we might share rides to the university, I driving one day, he the next.

"Oh," he said, "I don't plan on attending the class. In fact, I'm going to be away for most of the summer."

"I don't understand," I said.

"What's to understand? I'll take the book with me and just take comp [the comprehensive examination provided at the end of each of the school's core curriculum courses] in late August. No problem."

This was my first clue that everything about the University of Chicago was unlike anything I had previously known or even imagined about education. The place was sui generis, absolutely unique. This was owing to two things: to the nature of the education on offer and to the students it attracted. Distinguished from its founding in 1892 by William Rainey Harper, backed by Rockefeller money, the school's core curriculum was put in place by Robert Hutchins, who in 1929 at the age of thirty became president of the University of Chicago. No textbooks were allowed in the school's core courses. The examiner's office graded students, not their teachers. The notion of in loco parentis (the school taking up many of the duties of parents) was all but abandoned. Hutchins was no longer president of the university when I was a student there, but his program was firmly in place and the impress he had left upon it gave the school its character.

Students at the University of Chicago, at least the undergraduates among them, tended to be scraggly, almost militantly unkempt. I soon fell into that pattern myself, not shaving for two or three days in a row, sometimes wearing the same shirt more than once. I used to joke that the University of Chicago had only one quota—that on attractive women. David Brooks, the *New York Times* columnist, who was at the University of Chicago a few decades after me, in later years claimed while there to have majored in history and minored in celibacy. Women at Chicago, unlike at other universities of that day, were not there to catch husbands, or acquire a teaching certificate, but for something distinctly different.

That something different was an understanding of truth, beauty, and goodness. A high seriousness permeated the school. This was conveyed both in the classroom and through the not-so-hidden agenda that inspirited the place. This agenda held that getting a good job wasn't what education was about. As for jobs, the only worthy jobs were, in the University of Chicago's unspoken but clear message, that of artist (writer, composer, painter, sculptor), research scientist, and statesman, with the loophole being, fourth, a teacher of artists, scientists, and statesmen. Money, it was understood, must never become a central preoccupation. One might be a billionaire, but by the university's standard, if one weren't living the life of the mind, one was little more than a peasant raking gravel in the sun.

The University of Chicago radically changed my own values. After less than a year there, I no longer believed that success in life was marked by large bank accounts, handsome houses in approved neighborhoods, flashy cars. For roughly twenty or so years after leaving the university, in fact, I bought dullish cars on purpose—midrange Chevys, Oldsmobile Cutlasses—lest people think that the car as a status symbol could have any meaning for me. Only when Oldsmobile began to charge more than $20,000 for the Cutlass did I say screw it, and for a few grand more bought a BMW, and after that a series of S-Type Jaguars. I never looked back, except through the Jaguars' rearview mirrors.

Status itself, or so I told myself, was negligible: only intelligence, intellectual penetration, erudition mattered. My gestalt, a word I would not have used, or even known without the University of Chicago, had radically altered. The school had done away with all conventional forms of snobbery—of birth, wealth, good looks, social fluency—and the only snobbery that survived within its precincts was intellectual. I soon came to share in this snobbery, though my own intellectual snobbery was purely upward looking. I did not look down on people with scarce intellectual endowments or achievements. I continued above all—as I do to this day—to value a kind and generous heart. Besides, I myself had nothing to base my own intellectual snobbery on. Instead I looked up to those around me, teachers and students, who seemed dazzlingly brilliant, and longed one day to play in their ballpark.

The University of Chicago's intellectual cachet came as much from anywhere or anything as from those European intellectuals, Hitler's gift to America, who had fled Nazi Germany and found work at the university under Robert Hutchins. Theirs was the spirit that gave a cosmopolitan air to the place. The 1950s were still years in which Americans of any cultural pretensions looked to Europe as in every way superior to anything in the realm of culture that America had to offer. European art museums, symphony orchestras, writers, intellectuals, all seemed far in advance of anything available in the cultural or intellectual line in America.

Owing to my ignorance, I missed out on the great teachers of the day at Chicago, among them Joseph Schwab, Leo Strauss, Edward Shils. I attended some of the lectures of David Riesman. I went to poetry readings given by T. S. Eliot and Marianne Moore. I took an interesting class in modern poetry from the poet and critic Elder Olson. But it was less the classrooms than the readings and the general atmosphere of the school that put its deep stamp upon me.

I was not a notably strong student while at the University of Chicago. None of my teachers there whom I encountered in later years had any memory of me, and for the good reason that I rarely spoke in class and produced no distinguished work. My mind was elsewhere; it was on atmospherics more than actual content. In a Humanities 2 course, an instructor, flashing a famous painting on a screen, might tell the class where, given the painting's brushstrokes, our eye goes, but my eye never seems to have gone there. Another instructor might cite eight reasons for the Renaissance, but I was more interested in his accent than in those reasons. Other students were forthcoming in their classroom comments on the books we read, while I never spoke unless called upon, anxious at all times to hide my ignorance, which was extensive and deep.

My fellow students, many of them New Yorkers, were kids who appeared to have begun reading the *New Republic* and the *Nation* when they were twelve or thirteen. I imagined their families arguing about Trotsky, Max Shachtman, Nechayev. Many were Jewish. None was shy about setting out his or her opinions. I recall one day in class Elder Olson chanting a passage in French from Baudelaire and the girl sitting beside me joining him, in French and from memory. At that moment I wondered if I wouldn't have done better to study auto mechanics.

The university produced many a brilliant but oddly off-centered student. Three of its best-known graduates, all fewer than ten years older than I, were Susan Sontag, Allan Bloom, and Robert Silvers. A critic, a philosopher, an editor, all indubitably brilliant, yet each was without nuance and more than a touch humorless. None would have been the same had he or she not gone to the University of Chicago. All picked up its elevated spirit, none was quite able to remain sensibly grounded.

What I found most exhilarating at the university was the reading; none of it, as I noted, in textbooks. I was swept up by the elegance of Plato, the rigor of Aristotle, the analytical power of Thucydides, the subtlety of Tocqueville, the intellectual connections made by Max Weber, the philosophical tone of Freud in his *Civilization and Its Discontents.* I took a course in the novel that ran from *The Princess of Cleves* through Proust. I acquired a love for the culture of Greece and Rome. (One of my regrets is that I didn't major in classics.) I had nothing resembling a social life at the University of Chicago, only a reading life.

My first full year at the university I moved into a fraternity called Phi Kappa Psi. I call it a fraternity, but it was closer to a hot-sheet hotel. I was not a member of the fraternity, but then neither was the graduate student doing a PhD in biochemistry who lived there with his fiancée and his German shepherd, nor the fellow doing his residency in psychiatry who lived with a biracial dancer with the wonderful name of Arizona Williams, nor the six-foot-five Bob Bruhn, whose tuition was paid by the GI Bill after his service in Korea and who, while at the university, worked a full-time job at Commonwealth Edison.

I wound up living at Phi Psi because of a distant acquaintance named David Zimberoff, who was the president of the ramshackle fraternity and who suggested I share a three-room suite with him in its house on Fifty-Sixth and Woodlawn for a rent of $35 a month. A third person nearly shared these rooms with us, a remarkable young woman from Indianapolis named Dotti Cayton, who was David's inamorata and whom he married in his senior year. Dotti could have got into the university on the good-looking-female quota, but she was also excellent at school, able to get good grades without putting in long hours of study. David, who subsequently became a good friend, spent his evenings with Dotti, I mine attempting to catch up with all the reading I didn't do in the first nineteen years of my life. I didn't miss out on any social life, for the University of Chicago of that day offered none. I recall no dances, no parties, nor much in the way of dating among undergraduates. In later years a T-shirt turned up that read "The University of Chicago, Where Fun Goes to Die."

One academic quarter, I decided to stay up nights and sleep during days (my last class that quarter ended at noon). That gave me lots of time not only to read my assigned school readings but to fill in some of the contemporary or near contemporary authors I hadn't previously read: Hemingway, Fitzgerald, Faulkner, John O'Hara, and others. I began to read the *New Yorker*, which, I later realized, was going through one of its high periods, with such writers as A. J. Liebling, Edmund Wilson, Louise Bogan, William Maxwell, James Thurber, and E. B. White among its regular contributors.

That quarter I woke Bob Bruhn at 7:30 a.m. for his job. He slept in his clothes, shrugged upon being woke, put his feet in his combat boots, shrugged again, muttered thanks, and went off to work. Bruhn was a memorable storyteller. He once recounted for me escaping an inconveniently early returning husband, requiring him to gather up his trousers, shirt, and shoes, and leap, naked, all six foot five of him, from the bedroom's second-story apartment window. He once asked to use the phone in David Zimberoff's and my rooms, and I overheard him tell what I took to be his recently divorced wife that he had no need of any of the appliances from their home, nor of any of the furniture, nor of clothes he had left behind, nor of anything really, except he wondered if she still had his copy of the record of Walter Huston singing "September Song," which he would be grateful to have back. What became of Bob Bruhn I have no notion, though I hope a few good things.

Many years after leaving Chicago I had a call from a man named Robert E. Lucas, who, though I did not know it at the time, was a Nobel laureate in economics, asking if I would be willing to contribute to a Class of 1959 gift to the university. I recall saying to him that I hadn't realized the University of Chicago had "classes." One tended to arrive there at fifteen and depart at twenty-seven, as often as not without a degree.

Some former students never left Hyde Park, the University of Chicago neighborhood, which was an enclave of intellectual life in the otherwise philistine city of Chicago. Hyde Park seemed all bookstores, new and used, places to buy the then impressive *New York Times*, and German Jews who had shored up in Chicago among all the professors and students. The neighborhood was also, even as far back as the 1950s, slightly dangerous. To the south, across the Midway, was a Black neighborhood, to the north was a neighborhood containing many young Brandos and Presleys, or hood types. One night these hoods entered Phi Psi and began beating up any residents who happened to be around. Many were the stories of students getting beaten up crossing the Midway, which I came to think of as Apache territory. More than once I ran out of cigarettes late in the evening and was more than a touch nervous about walking a block or so away to Fifty-Fifth Street to buy another pack. A serious smoker, my addiction to nicotine trumped my fear. I took my chances and went out for smokes anyway, without, I'm pleased to report, harm.

After a year and a half at the university I had to declare a major. I had no aptitude for science; social science seemed to me somehow a touch dry. History was a possibility; philosophy wasn't. All that remained was English, and an English major I became. (In his story "Of This Time, of That Place," Lionel Trilling has a character tell the story's narrator that he was once an English major. "Really," the narrator replies, "in what regiment?") But there was a kicker to being an English major. This was that, in addition to the courses required, there was a junior-, then a senior-year list of extracurricular books, with forty or so titles on each list, that one was required to read and be tested on.

On the list were all those books that, left to one's own devices, one was likely not to read: *The Faerie Queene*, *Paradise Regained*, *Leviathan*, *The Pilgrim's Progress*, *Joseph Andrews*, and more. The idea behind the list, I take it, was, to call yourself an English major you ought to be acquainted with all the important books in English literature. I found I was not well organized enough to keep up with my regular coursework and read these books, too, and so I had to spend the summer between my junior and senior years reading the junior reading list. I left the University of Chicago without having taken my senior reading list exam, which I took roughly a year later, on a pool table at company headquarters, Fifth Armored Division, at Fort Hood Texas, monitored by a lieutenant from Alabama named James Bledsoe. My BA from the university couldn't have been more in absentia.

Sometime early in my last year at Chicago, walking through Harper Library, I made a fateful discovery, when for the first time I noticed the periodical racks. On those racks were such magazines, hitherto unknown to me, as *Partisan Review*, *Commentary*, the *Hudson Review*, the *Sewanee Review*, the *Antioch Review*, *Epoch*, the *Paris Review*, the *Kenyon Review*, the *Virginia Quarterly Review*, *Dissent*, the only recently begun English magazine *Encounter*, and I don't know how many others. The result was the intellectual equivalent of love at first sight. A bibliographical version of the gym rat, I began hanging out in the periodical room. I would eventually spend the better part of my life writing for such magazines.

"Little magazines" they were called—little because of their small circulations. Other magazines were journalism; the little magazines had pretensions—pretensions often fulfilled—to literature. One of the most influential among them, T. S. Eliot's the *Criterion*, is said never to have printed more than six hundred copies of an issue, yet in this magazine, whose life extended from 1922 to 1939, Eliot ran W. B. Yeats, Ezra Pound, Virginia Woolf, E. M. Forster, W. H. Auden, Hart Crane, and Luigi Pirandello. The *Criterion* also published Eliot's "The Waste Land," and was the first English-language magazine to publish Marcel Proust, Jean Cocteau, and Paul Valéry.

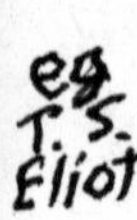

In the little magazines I came upon in Harper Library I discovered such writers as Lionel and Diana Trilling, Philip Rahv, Dwight Macdonald, Lionel Abel, Robert Warshow, Delmore Schwartz,

Midge Decter, Irving Howe, Sidney Hook, Norman Podhoretz, Elizabeth Hardwick, Saul Bellow, James Baldwin, Robert Lowell, H. R. Trevor-Roper, Hannah Arendt, Alfred Kazin, Bernard Malamud, Hilton Kramer, Leslie Fiedler, Isaiah Berlin, Mary McCarthy, and others. I could never hope to write like Plato or Herodotus, Plutarch or Polybius, or other of the authors in the University of Chicago curriculum, but perhaps it was possible to write as well as the contributors to the little magazines of the current day. For the first time I had the inkling that perhaps I might one day become a writer.

Around this time, I participated in my only extracurricular activity at the University of Chicago. I became a lowly subeditor on the *Chicago Review*, the school's own little magazine. The editor, a graduate student named Irving Rosenthal, assigned me the job of reading unsolicited manuscripts, most of them short stories, from the so-called slush pile. One day while doing so, Philip Roth, who was then in his twenties and an instructor in the English department, dropped in, well dressed and flush with the success of his recently published collection of stories, *Goodbye, Columbus*, his first and perhaps best book. Not long after my arrival at the *Chicago Review*, Irving Rosenthal in effect turned the magazine over to the publication of the works of Allen Ginsberg, William Burroughs, and other beat generation writers, which caused a minor scandal and eventually resulted in the firing of Rosenthal. I left the magazine around this same time, having contributed very little to it. But my brief period there set me to thinking about a career in literature, with editing a possible source of livelihood.

In the late 1960s, working as an editor at *Encyclopaedia Britannica*, I had a number of glancing encounters with Robert Hutchins, who was chairman of its board of editors. He was then in his late sixties, and,

I believe it fair to say, disappointed in his career. He had hoped to be appointed to the Supreme Court, a position that Franklin Roosevelt dangled before him without finally conferring it on him. Nothing after his glory years at the University of Chicago seemed to come of Hutchins's intellectual efforts. He first worked in New York for the Fund for the Republic and then departed for Santa Barbara, where he founded the posh Center for the Study of Democratic Institutions, jokingly referred to as the Leisure of the Theory Class. Tall, always perfectly turned out, a full head of white hair, a man who had more than his share of presence, his handsome face seemed to reflect his boredom and sadness both.

One day at a lunch at the Tavern Club in Chicago, I happened to be seated next to Robert Hutchins. At one point, he turned toward me, and, remarking that he understood that I had gone to the University of Chicago, asked, "Have they brought football back yet?"

"Not the last that I have heard," I replied.

What I regret failing to add was "And not at all, by the way, I owe you a vast debt of gratitude for what you did in reorganizing the University of Chicago along the lines of the highest intellectual seriousness. Under your influence the school radically changed my life and filled all my remaining days with unending interest. Thank you, sir."

Chapter Seven

You're Not Behind the Plow

Years before Frank Sinatra sang the song, my father told me that if I could make it in New York, I could make it anywhere. New York, which Saul Bellow once nicely described as a European city but of no known country, was then considered the American capital of art and talent generally. Since the University of Chicago had conferred upon me a (perhaps) exaggerated love of art and a longing to be thought talented, after leaving it, New York was my obvious destination.

With no clear plan in mind, before moving to New York, I wrote letters to the *New Yorker*, *Harper's*, and *Partisan Review*, informing them I was to be in their city and was available for job interviews at their convenience. Surprise, surprise, I heard back from none of them. Undaunted, I made the move anyhow. In New York I rented a large studio apartment on Willow Street in Brooklyn Heights. I had been told that W. H. Auden lived on Willow Street in Brooklyn Heights. Possibly Truman Capote did, too.

I discovered that New York had an employment agency devoted exclusively to editorial jobs. After enrolling with it, I was sent out on two interviews for possible jobs with trade magazines. In both cases I was asked if I had yet been either drafted or turned down by the military. When I answered neither, I was told that they were uninterested in me, for I was likely soon to be called up for military service. At another interview, this one for a trade magazine devoted to the pharmaceutical industry, I was one of roughly fifteen candidates awaiting an interview. I looked about at the doleful faces of my fellow job applicants and thought, *Why am I here, being interviewed for a job I have no interest in having?* and walked off.

Since I apparently was unable to make it in New York, I was less than confident that I could make it anywhere, so I returned to Chicago and had my name pushed up in the draft. In a month or so I received notice of a date for my physical. At the physical, all of us standing in our undershorts, next in line behind me was Leon Raine, a distant cousin, two years older than I, who had been second team All-State on the Senn High School football team. Leon, though not tall, was a *shtarker*, a strong man, who must have been fifty pounds heavier than I, every one of those pounds in well-formed muscle. I was found acceptable for military service; Leon, owing to his having a physician's note about his asthma, was not. I went off that afternoon in a bus to Fort Leonard Wood (known in those days as Fort Lost in the Woods), Missouri. Leon went home to dinner.

I marveled at how efficient the U.S. Army was in rounding up and taming its troops. In basic training, after being assigned to a barracks and had uniforms and other clothes distributed to us, everyone was sent to have his head shaved. Ducks' asses, crew cuts, Detroits, Tony

Curtises, standard Ivy League hairdos, it didn't matter what we went in with, we all came out alike, our style shorn from us in not much more than a minute per man. This had an impressively leveling effect.

Perhaps even more leveling were the three open toilets in the barracks' latrine. By open I mean that these toilets had no stalls. (Later, at clerk-typist school, stall walls were added, but only after clerk-typist school could one indulge in the luxurious privacy of using toilets behind doors.) This meant you had to defecate in the open, often with fellow troopers lined up in front of you impatiently awaiting the use of the toilet upon which you were sitting. I found I couldn't, so to say, perform under such conditions, and so arranged to wait until late at night to use the toilet most of my days at Leonard Wood.

Shaved heads, no bathroom privacy, sleeping in a crowded barracks among strangers, all these were first steps in the army's breaking one down and instilling a sense of one's own insignificance. Whatever one's status before entering the army—as an athlete, scholar, social adept, thug—that status was now divested of all meaning. As a totalitarian institution—that is, one that has total control over the people in it—the army had a remarkably high success rate in rehabilitating young offenders and even wayward jerks. In the army, you shaped up or, as they said, you shipped out. There really wasn't any alternative to shaping up but having your life permanently stained by a dishonorable discharge.

One was just another untrained soldier, at the mercy of officers, commissioned and especially noncommissioned. Once on KP, assigned with another trainee to scrub down an enormous black stove with Brillo pads, a sergeant with a quietly menacing look told us to cease talking or we would spend the entire night working on this stove. We had no reason to doubt him, and neither of us spoke again until the job was finished. One followed orders or paid heavily. Disobeying wasn't a possibility.

One of the things the army did for me was take me out of my comfortable but rather confining Jewish, upward-aspiring middle-class milieu. In my barracks there was Chester Cook, earnest in his Christian Science, who slept in the bunk above mine. There was Bobby Flowers, an Appalachian, better known in those days as a hillbilly, whose legs were terribly scarred from fire, but not sufficiently so to keep him out of the army, and whose first response when handed his M1 rifle was his laughing wish to use it on the wife who had recently divorced him. There was Jim Carson, from suburban Oak Park, who in later life became my insurance man. There was Johnson Bates, a Black man from Detroit, who early played the race card and whom in later years I put into a short story called "Race Relations" under the name Jackson Gates. There was a tall American Indian, or Native American as we now say, whose name I cannot recall but who impressed me with his stoical taciturnity. There was an almost hyper-friendly fellow named Wally Birmingham, who was liked by all. Amid this motley crew, I hear the strains of a song popular in that day and that seemed to play endlessly in the barracks, "Hang Down Your Head, Tom Dooley," sung by the Kingston Trio.

Among the noncommissioned officers, sergeants bearing more or less stripes who ruled our lives, the most prominent was a tall, slender Black man with a prominent Adam's apple named Andrew Atherton. Always in neatly pressed fatigues, an army ascot at his throat, boots burnished to a high shine, Sergeant Atherton combined formal language with profanity in an amusing way that resembled the character called the Kingfish on the old *Amos 'n' Andy* radio show. He instructed those of us of "the Hebrew persuasion" that it "behooved us to get our sorry asses to services on Friday nights." He told us it was "mandatory [sometimes pronounced 'malatory'] for every swinging dick" among us to straighten up his footlocker for inspection. During those rare moments of leisure allotted us, he might pop into the barracks and ask, "What are you young troopers doing in here, fucking the dog?"—canine copulation evidently his notion of a useless activity. Before joining the army, I later discovered, Sergeant Atherton, during the years when Blacks had few employment opportunities, had been a soda jerk in St. Louis. The army was a much more suitable place for him.

Apart from a week of bivouac, living in tents in the cold of the Missouri winter, I did not find basic training all that arduous. We drilled, we qualified on the rifle range with our weapons (never called guns), we jabbed at dummies with our bayonets, we tossed grenades, we did three chin-ups before going into the mess for meals. A time or two we filled our backpacks with forty or so pounds of weight, hoisted our rifles, and went off on ten-mile hikes. Cadence was called along the way—"Your job was there when you left, *your right*, your girl was there when you left, *your right.* Sound off, one, two. Sound off, three four. Cadence count. One two three four"—accompanied by dirty ditties: "I don't know, but I've been told, Eskimo pussy is mighty cold." "I know a girl in Kansas City, she has gumball on her titty."

On these marches I felt a strange sense of purely masculine pleasure. The pleasure derived from a military spirit that perhaps resides in most males, but is rarely called upon. This was the peacetime army, of course, and I have often since wondered how I would have done had I had to face enemy fire. How pleasing it would be to know, as I suspect every man wishes to know, that I had passed the test and could check the "No" box under cowardice.

The draft, which was legally halted in 1973, had much to recommend it. The draft not only redistributed the burden of the responsibility for fighting wars and engaging the nation in military conflicts in a more immediate and democratic way, but it tended to make the American electorate generally more thoughtful about foreign policy. All well and good to call for boots on the ground, but engaging in wars is viewed differently if some of those boots were to be filled by your own youthful children and grandchildren. A truly American military, inclusive of all social classes, would cause politicians and voters to be more selective in choosing which battles are worth fighting and at what expense. A draft army would also likely have the significant effect of getting the majority of the country behind those wars in which we do engage, as was the case in World War II, the last war the country was entirely behind.

The hiatus in one's life the draft brought could have a decisive effect on one's future. Certainly it did in my case. By drawing me at the age of twenty-two out of the workaday world for two years, the draft gave me space to think about my life and what I wanted to do with it. But for the draft, I might, God forfend, have gone to law school, simply out of the need to appear serious, and today have been a perhaps more prosperous but, I'm fairly certain, less contented man.

After eight weeks of basic training, I was sent to clerk-typist school at Fort Chaffee, Arkansas. Life became easier. Each morning, in fatigues, boots, and helmet liners, we marched off to class and were taught to type to the strains of the theme from *The Bridge on the River*

Kwai. I had taken typing in high school, but learned little from it, having spent most of the classes offered attempting to charm a girl seated next to me named Rochelle Malin. But now, hoping I would one day be a writer, which supplied me with a motive, I learned to type well and thereby acquired my one manual skill, which I used to think, if needs be, I could fall back on for employment.

Weekends we troopers were allowed to go into the town of nearby Fort Smith. We played poker at night in the barracks, and I, a steady winner at these games, treated my fellow players to dinner in town one Saturday night. On another occasion in town I saw Johnson Bates in the company of a notably stern sergeant, also Black, a man whose last name was Lewis. When I queried Bates about it, he replied oh, yeah, they were tight, and if there was anything he could do for me with Sergeant Lewis to let him know. I asked if his friend might have something to say about our next posting, and he said he'd look into it for me. The next day he told me that, for a hundred bucks, his friend could get me posted anywhere I pleased. "Anywhere in Europe would be great," I said, and handed over the money. Three weeks or so later, when our new assignments were posted on the company bulletin board, I discovered that I wasn't going to Europe but instead to Fort Hood, Texas. On the same posting it was noted that Johnson Bates was to have an honorable medical discharge. When I looked for Bates, he was already on his way back to Detroit, with my hundred bucks in his pocket. I was nicely conned, but, somehow, given the art with which it was done, felt it was worth it.

At Fort Hood, home of the Fifth Armored Division, I learned that I was not to work as a company clerk, the job for which I had been trained over the past eight weeks, but instead was assigned to the Public Information Office. The PIO was headed by a colonel named Marjorie Schulten, who drove a white Cadillac that she invariably referred to as "Paul." The office was run by the taciturn Sergeant MacLean, a tall, lean, unsmiling man clearly not to be fooled with.

The great comic figure in the office was an enlisted man named Carl Kerschler III. Kerschler was a graduate of the Wharton Business School. He had dark red hair, slightly buck teeth, blotchy skin, an ample chest, and drove a current-year black Cadillac convertible. Riding with him in it through the post, everyone assumed that no one less than a general, possibly even General Earle Wheeler, the post commander, would drive such a car, and saluted as we passed. Kerschler's specialty was an unhidden contempt for all things military. He wore his green uniform jacket in a one-button roll manner. His overemphatic salute suggested the phrase "Fuck you." The first of every month, he would say to me, "C'mon, time to go over and grovel for our pay," implying that our $88 monthly salary had no significance for him.

The post newspaper was published through the Public Information Office, and I was assigned to write for it. I wrote up stories of companies with perfect bond participation. I reviewed movies that were currently being shown on post, many of which I had not hitherto seen. Any drabs of culture that arose—one I recall was a story on the wife of a colonel who painted as a hobby—I covered. Occasionally I would take the week's paper—the *Fort Hood Armored Sentinel*—to the printer in Tyler, Texas. All this comprised what in that day was known as "good duty"—good because easy.

My barracks at headquarters company at Fort Hood was, unlike the wooden barracks at Leonard Wood and Chaffee, concrete with perhaps two hundred or so soldiers sleeping on its second floor. We enlisted men were awakened most mornings by a sergeant who banged a mop pole on the floor, and yelled, "Rise and shine, motherfuckers." While I was at headquarters company we were offered what was called "a good-conduct holiday" if the entire company could make it through a whole month with no car accidents or cases of venereal disease among us. We never made it.

Large and impersonal though headquarters company was, I managed to make two friends there. One is Tom Anderson, with whom I worked at the PIO and who went on to become a legal scholar. The other, Freddy Schindler—New York, Jewish, gay—worked for the post's Catholic chaplain, to whom he never referred as other than "Big Daddy." I've stayed in touch with Tom through the decades. Freddy I met one day on Fifth Avenue in Manhattan, with a young woman with whom he worked as a window designer and who, upon being introduced to me, asked if I were "Epstein the furrier," which got a good laugh out of Freddy.

Apart from the brothels across the border in Juárez, which I took a pass on, there wasn't a lot to do off post at Fort Hood. The nearby small town of Killeen, Texas, provided little beyond the prospects of a beer and a tattoo. Austin was too far away, though I spent a weekend there and another in what seemed to me a dullish Dallas. I had more than a year to serve on my two years, and it looked to be a long, slow one.

So when I learned that there were clerkships available in recruiting stations in Little Rock, Arkansas, and Shreveport, Louisiana, I applied. The first sergeant at headquarters company told me that I had been chosen for one and to walk over to Company B to discuss the details with a staff sergeant there named Henderson.

Henderson turned out to be a man with a strong southern accent who, I sensed, was not long on patience. "So what do you want, Little Rock or Shreveport?" he asked. I realized I had a nanosecond to answer. I thought Shreveport, being in Louisiana, probably had better food and a more tolerant atmosphere, but Little Rock was closer to Chicago and the scene only two years earlier of the political tumult that was the integration of the town's Central High School. "Little Rock, Sergeant," I answered, and a fateful answer it turned out to be. In Little Rock, I met my first wife, with whom I had two children. I have often wondered since how different my life might have been had I said, "Shreveport, Sergeant."

Chapter Eight

Good Duty

As the bus from Fort Hood pulled into the Greyhound station in Little Rock, I was feeling immensely pleased at my good fortune. Little Rock did have a nearby air force base, but it had no army post. This meant that I would be able to live in an apartment, away from the round-the-clock military discipline, the mediocre food, the sharing of sleeping quarters with two hundred strangers. My job at the recruiting station was strictly nine-to-five, with weekends my own. Somehow it all seemed, as Omar Khayyam had it, "paradise enow."

I spent my first night in Little Rock at the YMCA. The next morning I scuttled about to find an apartment. What I found was a studio, one large room, with light coming in from both sides, with a double bed that rolled out of a closet, a few comfortable chairs, a small table to dine upon, a bathroom, and a small kitchen. The apartment backed on to the governor's mansion, whose current occupant was the obstreperous Orval Faubus, who did his best to prevent Black kids from integrating the city's Central High School. Less than a block away was a Safeway supermarket. Perhaps best of all, as I was soon to discover, a block or so to the east on Main Street, was a space taking up perhaps four or five empty lots, where under ample tents and with some regularity various religious revivalist meetings were held.

The revivalist meetings, which I often attended standing on the outside edge of the tents, entailed the laying on of hands and talking in tongues, and these constituted my occasional evening entertainment. One evening a heavyset woman came out of one of these meetings and said to me, "Won't you come in? He died for you." Which chilled me enough to keep me away for a full week.

Apart from its stove and refrigerator, my apartment was without appliances. I had no television set, radio, or telephone. I chiefly ate sandwiches, Campbell's soups, and cereal. I made the useful discovery that I had a taste—a gift?—for solitude. I not only didn't mind being alone for long stretches but rather enjoyed it. I passed much of the time reading and attempting to write short stories on a small portable Olivetti typewriter I had bought for $25 from a sergeant at Fort Hood in need of cash. I took books out of the main branch of the Little Rock library, which was between my apartment and the recruiting station. Weekends could seem a bit lengthy, so at one point I bought a basketball and dribbled three or four blocks away to an always-empty schoolyard, where I shot baskets. Some weekend nights I walked the eight or nine blocks to downtown Little Rock to see a movie. Most nights, though, I read for four or five hours: novels, biography, history.

The book I remember most vividly from those days is a collection of Sidney Hook's essays, *Political Power and Personal Freedom*, which changed my less-than-fully-formed politics. A liberal veering onto radicalism, I was against the spread of nuclear weapons, against the harsh and immoral segregation laws still in play in Little Rock and elsewhere in the South, for labor unions, for what I thought greater economic justice, for wider tolerance generally. Hook's book, so impressive was its arguments, converted me to an anti-communist liberal.

I met Sidney Hook many years later, and his first words on meeting me were "I expected a fatter man." When I asked why fatter, he responded, "Because in your writings you are frequently funny. I think of funny men as fat, you know, like Falstaff." Sidney took to calling me, for some reason usually on Saturday evenings. He was then living on the West Coast, where the time was two hours earlier than the Midwest. When I first asked Sidney about what I knew to be his fragile health, in a raspy voice he replied, "What do you want, an organ recital?" Once, when Hannah Arendt's name came up, he remarked that, brilliant though she might be, she was wrong about everything important. "But the gang around *Partisan Review* were taken in by her panoply of German classical learning," he said. "Not that those fellows were so smart. I had to argue them into being for World War Two."

I liked well enough the guys I worked with at the recruiting station, but, apart from our lunches together at nearby restaurants and the occasional beer after work, I felt no need to socialize with them, nor they, apparently, with me. All, like me, were draftees, apart from a marine sergeant named Jackie Taylor and an air force private from Alabama, Franklin, whose first name is now lost to me. One of my fellow typists was by training a landscape architect, and gay, though not out of the closet. (I only learned of his gaiety from a woman who told me she saw him necking with a man at a party.) The sergeant in charge of us was Wilson Duncan, a genial man who needed to step out from time to time for a drink. Physicals were administered by a young physician, Captain G. L. Holister, who, against American Medical Association rules of those days, drove a sports car and on weekends made house calls to civilians for which he charged $7. When he passed us in the hall, we generally greeted him with two quick hernia coughs. He took it in good humor.

My job, working in a room with three other soldiers and an older evangelical woman, was to type up the results of Dr. Holister's physicals. The physicals themselves revealed odd, sometimes strange facts about the physical conditions of young men who lived back in the Arkansas hills, some of whom were missing most of their teeth, or, unbeknownst to them, had venereal diseases, or came from towns with such names as Toad Suck. I was rarely called on to type up more than ten or so of these physicals a day. Owing to the lack of work, from time to time Sergeant Duncan would tell one or the other of us typists to knock off for the day at noon.

I early discovered a newspaper and magazine store on Main Street, which carried the English *Spectator* and *New Statesman* and a rather grim-looking biweekly called the *New Leader*. One of the first issues of the *New Leader* I read contained a debate between Bertrand Russell and Sidney Hook over the question of whether it would be better to be Red, for which read Russian communist, or Dead, for which read killed in a war against the communists. Russell argued more elegantly for the better-to-be-Red side, but Hook, arguing it was better to be a dead lion than a live jackal, ultimately won. Other contributors to these *New Leader* issues included Irving Kristol, Diana Trilling, Daniel Bell, and a film critic I hadn't heard of before named Manny Farber.

To the *New Leader* I sent my first article, a piece about life among the races in Little Rock roughly two years after the 1957 Little Rock Central High School integration crisis. A piece of roughly 1,500 words, which contained perhaps eight hundred pretensions, it was—lo, wow, pow!—accepted by the magazine's managing editor, a man named Moshe Decter. I walked around with that letter in my pocket for the better part of a week, taking it out to reread it whenever the occasion allowed. A thrill is defined as "a sudden feeling of excitement and pleasure"; my own feeling at the acceptance of my article at the *New Leader* was two stages beyond that.

After receiving my letter from Moshe Decter, I began to wonder how much money I would be paid for my article: $200, $500, perhaps an even $1,000? Two weeks went by, then three, and, my patience run out, I wrote to the magazine's editor in chief, a man listed on the masthead as S. M. Levitas, that there had been more than one theft in the mailboxes in the building in which I lived (a lie, of course) and I wondered if his check for my article might have been stolen. Levitas wrote back to tell me that, as a young man, perhaps I was unaware that "the truth has no price tag. The *New Leader* does not pay its contributors. But I am here to encourage you to do more writing."

One of the more congenial places in the Little Rock of those days was the offices of the *Arkansas Gazette*. The paper had won a Pulitzer Prize for its courageous stand on behalf of integration during the Central High School crisis. I cannot now remember the subject, but I sent a letter to the editor, perhaps attacking some position or other of my neighbor Governor Faubus, which I carried by hand to the paper's office. There I met a man named Jerry Neil, who soon became a friend. Jerry was said to have written many of the editorials for which Harry Ashmore, the paper's editor, received most of the credit. Jerry must have been twenty-five years older than I, but from our first meeting he took me seriously. In what will become a pattern, a leitmotif, in my life, Jerry Neil was another older man who befriended and encouraged me.

Not that I saw Jerry Neil regularly. Apart from at lunch, neither did I ever see him socially. His wife drove him to work from their home in North Little Rock. A drinking man, he did not himself drive. He came to the *Arkansas Gazette* early and wrote out his quite brilliant editorials before lunch. "Who has it better than I?" he once told me. "I start out the day telling our governor he is a major-league jerk, I instruct General de Gaulle, Harold Macmillan, and others to calm down and stay on the job, then I break for lunch, where I stay just sober enough to come back to the office to paste up letters for the next day's paper, then it's home again for dinner and drinks." The word was that the *New York Herald Tribune*, felt to be the most sophisticated American newspaper of that day, was keen to have Jerry Neil work for it, but, for whatever complex of reasons, he didn't want to leave Arkansas.

Jerry lunched at the bar-restaurant in the Marion Hotel called the Gar Hole, so named after a garfish that swam about in a tank over the bar. The Gar Hole was where I met my first wife, who worked as a waitress there. She was born in Batesville, Arkansas; her father a stonemason, a southern good ole boy, a drinker with a freezer full of dead squirrels he had shot. Her mother, a shy woman, was a seamstress who made the uniforms for the local high school's marching band.

She, my future wife, had become pregnant in high school, and had her first child at the age of seventeen, marrying the man who had made her pregnant. She had a second child with him. Then, after he had gone into the navy, they divorced, and she remarried, this time to a man, also in the navy, from Montana, a marriage lasting not much longer than two years. While living with her second husband in Virginia, her first husband's family went to court to gain custody of the couple's two sons, which they did. In Little Rock, she was living with a slightly older sister and her sister's husband, who drove a truck delivering potato chips and other snack food to small towns in Arkansas.

I sensed she had come on to me twice. The first time was when I was at lunch with Jerry Neil, the second time was after work when I was having a beer with a few guys from the recruiting station. On the second occasion, after departing from my drinking companions, I returned to the Gar Hole and asked if she were free that evening. She said she was off duty at 10:00 p.m. We agreed to meet in the lobby of the Marion Hotel.

I knew little of nightlife in Little Rock, so I suggested we go back to my apartment. I opened a bottle of wine, and there we sat, perhaps thirty feet apart, and talked from 10:30 p.m. or so until 7:30 a.m., when I had to dress for work at the recruiting station. We talked, as I recall, mostly about her, the complications and sadness of her life. She explained how she had lost custody of her two sons, Lynn and David, who were now ten and eight. She told me that her divorce from her second husband, a man named Mitchell Hart, was in process. We shared some laughter. The flow of conversation was easy, and thoroughly enjoyable. (Years later, she said that I had said something on our first night together that led her to know she could trust me, and I, foolishly, never pressed her on what it was.) I rolled my bed out of the closet for her and watched her slowly undress as I left for work. We agreed to see each other later that evening.

And so we did, and did again for the next three nights. The fourth night we slept together. In our hyper-candid age, I suppose I ought here to describe in some detail our sex. But, even though my first wife has been dead for more than a decade now, I find I cannot. All I can say, as I have a character in a short story say after sleeping with a woman he long fantasized about, "I did not want my money back." I hope she, my wife, felt the same.

Ten or so days later, on a weekend afternoon, she showed up at my studio apartment, suitcase in hand, announcing that she would like to move in. I didn't object. She continued to work at her job; I still had six months or so to go on my two-year army hitch. One day she announced that her divorce from her second husband had come through. We celebrated with a steak dinner. At the time I had no notion that I would be her third husband. As with cats, so with husbands and wives, it is probably not a good idea to have more than two; if three, after all, why not have four or five? I believe she, my first wife, ended up with five husbands. When it comes to marriage, some women are better closers than others, and a good closer my first wife evidently was.

What clinched the marriage for me was her announcement one day not long after she had moved into my apartment that she was pregnant. All the signs were there, including, she told me, the morning sickness that accompanied the birth of her two earlier sons. Abortion was still at the back-alley, kitchen table stage, and I wasn't about to tell her to get one. I knew such a marriage would upset my parents, but I could not bring myself to tell her that if she needed any help packing, I would be glad to lend a hand. I was then twenty-three, a fairly standard age in my generation for men to marry. We married one day, during my lunch break, at the office of a justice of the peace in downtown Little Rock. When I came out I had a parking ticket. Not a good omen.

My parents, especially my father, were opposed to the marriage. At the heart of my father's opposition was my marrying so quickly and also outside my religion. My mother kept her own counsel on the subject. I told neither of them that behind my marriage was the pregnancy of my wife, though they may well have guessed and would soon enough discover it. I also sensed that my father was too kindly a man to maintain his anger at me for long. For a time, though, we ceased communication. I wrote to ask my mother to send me the $1,650 that I received as an inheritance from an uncle of my father's, with a portion of which I bought a ten-year-old, stick-shift, green Ford sedan.

The marriage lasted nearly a decade. Alas, it was never a strong one. My wife spent her days cooking and shopping for antiques. She loved animals, and at one point we had a household with two dogs and five Siamese cats. But something was missing from her life. I thought it was her lost children. Not long after we married, I went to court to get her the visitation rights for her sons that she had never acquired after her divorce from her first husband. Later, after her first husband had remarried to a mean-spirited woman, and the boys, then twelve and ten years old, visited us in New York looking much the worse for wear, I arranged to have their father served with a subpoena, and in court won full custody of them for her.

I thought, mistakenly, that I, fine and heroic fellow that I am, was putting her life back together for her. At one point, I moved with her to a Chicago suburb in which lived two of her first cousins from Arkansas, both contemporaries—one married to a man who ran a mini-supermarket selling Italian food, the other to a man who worked for him—but that, too, didn't much move the needle of her unhappiness. I have since come to the bleak view that she probably never loved me—not in the complete way I have since come to know. Quite possibly, given the harsh circumstances of her early life—parents without understanding, a want of education, an early pregnancy—she was unable to love at all, or at least not for long.

The weakness of the marriage was owing quite as much to me as to her. Whether it makes more sense to marry older, when one's ambition has cooled, or young, when passions are heated, is an unresolvable question. (Married or single, a non-Zen koan runs, neither is a solution.) In this marriage we shared humor, and the sex was pleasurable, but true intimacy somehow eluded us. I encouraged her to go to college, take a degree in any subject she wished, but she wasn't interested. I wanted happiness for her—what man doesn't want to bring happiness to his wife—but wasn't finally able to deliver it.

I, meanwhile, had too much going on in my own life. Once out of the army, I needed to find a job. I also needed to continue writing, which meant further hours spent reading. I am one of those fellows for whom work comes first—always had been, still am. A full-time husband or, for that matter, full-court press father, I could never be. Asked what phrase my children might have heard most frequently from me when they were growing up, my guess is that it might be "I'll be there as soon as I finish this paragraph."

After less than a decade together, my wife and I divorced. I have since come to think—too charitably to myself?—that perhaps my wife brought too much baggage to our marriage. Her first pregnancy while still in high school could not in any way have been easy. I don't know this for a certainty, but my guess is that she is the one who walked away from all of her marriages. Freedom, not security, was the name of her desire—the freedom she missed out on as a teenager. In support of this theory, when we agreed to separate, I assumed that she would take her two older boys with her, leaving me with my (by now) two sons with her. Not at all. She demanded that I take all four boys, arguing that if I wouldn't agree to this then she would take all four, thus depriving me of my own biological children. I took custody of all four. Besides, by now I had come to love my two stepsons, to whom life thus far had been so cruel.

As for the details of my divorce, they, I suppose, could be said to have been made in heaven. For one thing, it was uncontested; for another, I paid no regular alimony, though in the early years of our separation, I sent my now ex-wife fairly regular payments of five or six hundred dollars. Before she left I also bought her a new yellow Volkswagen Bug. (She asked if I minded paying a few dollars extra for a leather steering wheel.) My attorney, Samuel Freifeld, a high school pal of Saul Bellow's, charged me only $500 for his associate's courtroom appearance at the divorce proceedings. When after the divorce trial I went out for a drink with my two witnesses, each during the trial attesting to what a fine father I was, one, a witty man named Martin Self, who would die in his forties, said they must run along, pretending that they were professional witnesses and had two other trials to attend. I returned to my four sons, wondering what to make them for dinner.

My now long ex-wife, later married to a retired air force sergeant named Monte Shields, had a fifth son, Matthew, born badly brain-damaged. Unable to speak, needing to be fed, his vision uncertain, he lived on to the age of twenty-eight, with his father his main caregiver. After Monte, a good man by every reckoning, died, my ex-wife, unable to cope with the boy on her own, placed him in an institution. She herself died not long after this sad son did, in a recovery room after an operation for rectal cancer. Some people can't catch a break, and she, poor woman, was one of them.

Chapter Nine

Among the Mensheviks

After my discharge from the army, I returned to Chicago with my new, and newly pregnant, wife. We lived for a week or so in my parents' apartment, then found one of our own, furnished, in a building off Sheridan Road called the Sherwin Arms. We soon thereafter moved into a one-bedroom apartment on Seeley Avenue in West Rogers Park and began collecting our own furniture.

To bring in some income while scrambling around for a job, I worked for a month or so for my father, partly as a shipping clerk, partly sitting for hours stamping out the plates for ID bracelets. I was looking for editorial work, which in Chicago was less than abundant. A job on either of the two metropolitan dailies—the *Chicago Tribune* and the *Sun-Times*—was unlikely, for neither paper any longer hired anyone who did not go to journalism school. There was something called the City News Bureau, where the investigative journalist Seymour Hersh, with whom I went to the University of Chicago, began his journalistic career, but it paid the hopeless salary of $45 per week. *Time* and *Newsweek* had Chicago bureaus, but they both hired out of New York. An inquiry I sent to *Chicago* magazine went unanswered. I interviewed for a job as an assistant editor at the *Kiwanis Magazine*, and got it.

A strange place to begin, the *Kiwanis Magazine*, at least for a young man who now fancied himself an intellectual, a highbrow, even an avant-gardist. Sinclair Lewis had long before mocked the middle-class Rotarian spirit in his novel *Babbitt*, and the Kiwanis were a notch below the Rotarians. But I needed the income and, at twenty-three, to be out on my own.

The job called for me to write up the activities of various Kiwanis club activities around the country, their pancake breakfasts, peanut-day campaigns, good works generally. Under the magazine's chief editor, a genial man fifteen or so years older than I named Dick Gosswiller, I learned how to lay out a magazine. I was able at one point to convince Dick to let me publish an essay in the *Kiwanis Magazine* on Henry Adams, which must surely have been among the least read pieces ever run in the magazine.

A notable character at the *Kiwanis Magazine* was Bob Lamb, who had hired on around the time I did as the magazine's advertising-space salesman. Twenty or so years older than I, he had earlier worked for *Architectural Digest* and was a man who enjoyed his booze. He told me that his work and drinking went hand in hand. During his *Architectural Digest* days, he would be selling the board of some ad agency on space in the magazine when, even though it was a done deal, some twenty-six-year-old twit would offer the most hopeless objections. He responded, patiently, thoughtfully, kindly—and needed three or four drinks afterward to calm himself down.

Bob Lamb used to take a longish morning break at the Boul-Mich bar off Michigan Avenue, there to have a drink or two. I would occasionally join him. Often at the bar was Wendell Smith, a sportswriter for the *Chicago Tribune*, a man who was one of the many claimants to being the inventor of the jump shot in basketball, and who volunteered that he fixed Ernie Banks up with a hooker whom Banks went on to marry. (One sometimes meets the most interesting people in bars at ten thirty in the morning.) I have no notion of what became of Bob Lamb. Like most serious drinkers, I assume he was not long-lived, but life with him was never dull.

I encountered my first and only known anti-Semitism at the Kiwanis office. I was at the time attempting to learn Russian—I didn't—and would occasionally bring a small Russian primer along with me on coffee breaks. On one occasion, an older man, in charge of new membership in the organization, asked what I was reading. When I told him I was trying to learn Russian, he nodded in an odd way. He later spread the rumor that I was a (Jewish implied) communist. Nothing, really, came of it.

I stayed at the the *Kiwanis Magazine* for more than a year. While there, Mark, my first son, was born. My wife's ob-gyno was a man named David Turow, the father of the novelist Scott Turow. Dr. Turow delivered babies only on Tuesdays, which he was able to arrange through the use of induced labor. I sat with four other Turow fathers, awaiting the births of our children, wondering if we shouldn't arrange a pool on whose child would be delivered first. My son was born perfectly healthy, and turned out to be, as he would throughout his boyhood and youth, a baby who caused the least trouble, and required the least help from his parents.

After a year or so at the *Kiwanis Magazine*, I learned an editorial job had become available at the *New Leader* in New York. After my first published article there, I had written a few reviews for the magazine. I applied and got the job. The salary was $6,000 a year, and, despite the magazine's socialist character, with no health insurance or any other benefits included. For $250 per issue, I also edited an academic quarterly called *Labor History*, bringing my salary up to $7,000. In those distant days, if one could earn an annual salary of $10,000 it seemed one's financial worries were over. I moved to New York in advance of my wife and newborn son.

The *New Leader* was a socialist, anti-communist magazine, whose founding editor, S. M. Levitas, was said to have briefly been the Menshevik deputy mayor of Vladivostok. A man who smoked two packs of cigarettes a day without ever buying any, Sol Levitas was a famous and artful *schnorrer*, Yiddish for "beggar." Subeditors were said to come into his office asking for a raise and departing without the raise but with a review copy of a book in which they had no interest.

In its rare advertisements, the *New Leader* carried the blurb: "Of all the magazines that cross my desk, the one I should most sorely miss would be *The New Leader*." The blurber was T. S. Eliot. How, I wondered, did Levitas get it? One day I went to the office files and took out the Eliot folder. In it I discovered that Levitas, who knew Eliot's importance, but seems not to have had the faintest notion of his interests, attempted to get Eliot to review books for the *New Leader*. Each time not Eliot but his secretary wrote back to say thanks but no thanks. Levitas, meanwhile, assumed a personal relationship had developed between him and Eliot. One day he wrote to Eliot to say that he, Sol Levitas, and his wife were going to be in London and would like nothing better than to "break bread" (the words in the letter were underlined) with Eliot and his wife. Eliot for some reason agreed, and at the meal they shared in London, Levitas got his blurb. But, then, I have never heard a story about T. S. Eliot, famous for his poems' anti-Semitism, that didn't show him to be a kindly and decent man, not least to Jews.

My first week in New York I stayed with a man named Alfred Sundel, who had published a single short story in *Partisan Review*—a grand achievement in those days—and, of much less prestige, later adapted more than twenty books for *Classics Illustrated,* better known as Classic comics. With the help of two female cousins, nieces of my father's, I found a two-bedroom apartment in a new building in Flushing, Queens. Manhattan, even then, was too expensive for a family man on my salary.

The *New Leader*'s office was at 7 East 15th Street, just west of Union Square and east of Fifth Avenue. The building also housed the library of the Socialist Party of America's Rand School and on its upper floors the New York headquarters of the International Association of Machinists. The Tamiment Institute, which ran a summer camp in the Poconos for workers and which supplied much of the financial backing for the magazine, was on the ground floor. The head of the Tamiment Institute in those days was an Eastern European immigrant named Ben Josephson, who once complained to me about Max Eastman, at the camp in the Poconos, running around naked "with his *farkakte* balls," a phrase and picture one doesn't easily forget.

The magazine had two offices across the hall from each other, one for editorial, one for business. Two other editors, both New Yorkers born, worked on the magazine: Myron Kolatch was then its managing editor and Joel Blocker its associate editor. (Associate editor was also my title.) Myron Kolatch, an Orthodox Jew, was a man who made it plain that you were unlikely to tell him anything he didn't already know. Joel Blocker had published a review or two in *Commentary*, knew Hebrew well enough to bring out a book of translations of Israeli short stories, and, one readily sensed, was not altogether happy in his job. In fact, he had been looking for another job well before I arrived. Dark, handsome, gifted at foreign languages, a graduate of the University of Chicago, Joel came to work an hour or so late four days a week. The reason, I discovered, was that he was in psychoanalysis, four sessions a week. (In those days a session cost $25.)

A number of people in New York I knew from those days were in psychoanalysis. Not to be psychoanalyzed even suggested that one was more than a touch fearful to look into the darkness of one's own psyche. Analysts held great power over analysands. At one point Joel told me that he had wanted to marry an attractive woman he was seeing, but his analyst told him it was not a good time for him to enter into a marriage. Eighteen or so months later, the woman married someone else, which prompted Joel to feel that his analyst was correct in cautioning him against the marriage.

Diane Ravitch worked part-time at the magazine without, I suspect, salary. Diane, who went on to write a history of the New York public schools and other books on education, was born in Houston, went to Wellesley, married Richard Ravitch, scion of a wealthy real estate developer—her husband would for a year (2009–10) serve as lieutenant governor of New York—and had strong but still unformed intellectual yearnings. She also had a lovely sense of humor. On the days when she came in, there was laughter, at least shared between the two of us. She was excellent at inventing comic titles for book reviews. One I remember, a review of a complaining memoir by an East Indian woman named Sabvalah, was "Days of Whine and Neuroses." (It was rejected by the humorless Myron Kolatch.) Diane was amused at my reading the title of one of our lead articles, "Agonizing Opportunity in South East Asia," in the voice of Lauren Bacall. She also enjoyed my standing up at my desk over the far-from-clear copy of the aged Reinhold Niebuhr and singing, "C'mon, Reiny, let's do the Twist."

My job at the *New Leader* was chiefly to edit the articles and reviews sent in by the magazine's contributors, many of whom were Germans or Russians not yet fully in command of English. Among them were Walter Laqueur, George Lichtheim, Boris Nicolaevsky. A few English Labor Party MPs—Denis Healey, David Marquand—wrote for the magazine, sending in handwritten copy that needed no editing at all. During the two years I was at the *New Leader*, I did no writing of my own. On occasion I rewrote other people's articles. In one instance, I rewrote a brief piece by an old socialist named William Bonn, which drew a letter from Dwight Macdonald, whom I then much admired, citing it as a classic. Macdonald's letter gave me much pleasure, though of course of a secondary sort, for I could not tell him or anyone else that I had written the piece.

I often went to lunch with Joel Blocker, and we were occasionally joined by Albert Goldman, the magazine's music (chiefly jazz) critic. Al Goldman was ten years older than I, and then teaching at the School of General Studies at Columbia, which he referred to as "working the lounge at Columbia." His conversation was a blend of jazz slang and psychoanalytic jargon. Once, before reading the galley proof of one of his pieces in the *New Leader* office, he asked if I would mind dimming the lights, turning on some gentle music, and bringing him a box of Kleenex, the joke here of course being his intention to masturbate while reading his own writing. Another time, I was in his apartment on Lexington Avenue, when I noted the photograph of an attractive woman whom he told me was his former fiancée. When I remarked that she seemed so young, he replied that the secret to remaining youthful-looking is to stay immature.

Al wrote books on Lenny Bruce, Elvis, and John Lennon, and was working on a book on Jim Morrison of the Doors at his death by heart attack in 1994 at the age of sixty-six. I had edited a scholarly book he wrote on plagiarism in Thomas De Quincey, but I had moved back to Chicago by the time he was working on his Lenny Bruce book (*Ladies and Gentlemen—Lenny Bruce!!*), on which he asked me to help him by interviewing a Rush Street pharmacist who supplied Bruce with drugs when he performed in Chicago, which I did. Al praised Lenny Bruce, whom he thought a shaman of sorts, but took down both Elvis and Lennon in his biographies of them. So strong were his takedowns of these rock idols that others criticized Al in the lyrics of their own songs. Elton John said of him, "Albert Goldman is human vermin." Had Sir Elton said that about me, I would strongly consider using it as a blurb on all my own books.

John Simon signed on as the *New Leader*'s film critic not long after I began working on the magazine. As a critic, he soon achieved the reputation of a professional killer. He would later review three of my books with pleasing generosity; though, characteristically, he found a few grammatical errors in them (I once wrote that John could find a grammatical error in a stop sign). John's first movie review for the *New Leader* was of *David and Lisa*, a film about two mentally troubled adolescents, a review that concluded that, doubtless, the Lacedaemonians were correct in burying deformed children. On one occasion John told me that Pauline Kael told him that he was quite wrong about one of his movie reviews, but that she nonetheless admired its style. "Dear me," John replied to her, "I had no notion you had the least interest in style."

Stanley Edgar Hyman, who worked at the *New Yorker* and taught at Bennington and was best known as a critic of critics, wrote each issue of the magazine's leading book review. His occasional visits to the office, usually staying on for lunch, were events of much pleasant talk, gossip, jokes. At a party at Joel Blocker's, I met Isaac Bashevis Singer, who had not yet attained his worldly fame.

But mine was far from the literary life. My life was mostly lived in Queens, in our apartment in Flushing. I recall picking up my wife and infant son at LaGuardia, where they arrived from Arkansas, and she wearing a mink stole my mother had given her. We repaired to our apartment and napped, the three of us, naked on our bed. My wife was pregnant with our second child. (Have I neglected to mention that I was national chairman of the Unplanned Parenthood Committee?) In our building lived a couple, Sandy and Lenny Kleiderman, with whom we became good friends. Such social life as my wife and I had was with the Kleidermans. Lenny wanted to make movies; Sandy's twin sister, Ilene, was going with and would marry the novelist Leslie Epstein, whose father and uncle were screenwriters (of, among other flicks, *Casablanca*), and whose own son Theo, decades later, would become the baseball guru who would bring World Series victories to both the Boston Red Sox and the Chicago Cubs.

The hours at the *New Leader* were long. At the end of my first year at the magazine, Mike Kolatch called me in to thank me for working as hard and as well as I did and told me he was giving me a $600 (a year!) raise, and wished it could be more. Joel, he added, was disappointing, and probably looking for another job. Not long after this, Joel, at lunch, confessed to me that in fact he was looking for another job. He added that Kolatch had given him a measly $1,000 raise, which caught my attention. Joel left not long after, getting a job at *Newsweek.* I myself soon began looking for a new job.

One day in the office, not long after Joel Blocker had left the magazine, Kolatch asked Hilton Kramer, who wrote occasional pieces of art criticism for the magazine, if he knew anyone who would be interested in Joel's job.

"As it happens, I do," Hilton replied. "Me." He was hired on the spot.

Hilton had worked as an editor at *Arts Magazine* and as the art critic for the *Nation*, though in recent years he had been freelancing. Not an easy thing to do, freelancing, not if one is a highbrow critic of unrelenting high standards, which Hilton was. He would later tell me about getting checks for contributions, written out in hand, for $22 for pieces for *Commonweal* magazine. Unlike the often sulking Joel Blocker, Hilton was a man of high spirits, with a keen sense of the absurdity of the world. In his strong New England accent, he used such words as "lavish," "shameless," "oeuvre" with a comic emphasis. Working in the same room with him was a delight.

Hilton was nine years older and much more advanced intellectually than I, though our rapport was immediate and remained complete throughout his life. We went to lunch his first full day at the *New Leader*, and I spoke with him candidly about how things worked at the magazine. We laughed a lot and found many of the same things amusing. He was soon one of my dearest friends.

Bourgeois in his habits—he wore elegant neckties, Brooks Brothers suits, serious hats, was well-groomed, punctual—he was nonetheless bohemian in spirit, the inheritance perhaps of his association with so many visual artists. Not long after he came to work at the *New Leader*, he arranged for my wife and me to be invited to dinner at the loft in Hoboken of Esta Leslie, whom he would soon marry. Esta was a consummate cook, but what I remember most about the dinner was being seated in a perfect position to face a life-size nude painting of Esta abed done, in realistic figurative mode, by her ex-husband, Alfred Leslie.

Hilton was someone who knew only to speak his mind. In later years, he was on the editorial board of the *American Scholar* magazine when the subject came up of who was the best person to write about the question of whether psychoanalysis was interested in "cure." Diana Trilling, herself a great votary of psychotherapy, suggested the name of a then popular psychologist named Robert Coles. "Let me assure you," Hilton retorted, "Robert Coles has no interest in cure." At another meeting, when the political scientist Edward Luttwak provided an elaborate exegesis of deconstruction, Hilton, in a voice loud enough to be heard round the table, said, "Brilliant, quite wrong of course, but absolutely brilliant." At a four-man symposium at Northwestern University on the subject of modernism, after Erich Heller, Richard Ellmann, and a professor-painter named George Cohen finished speaking, Hilton rose to say that "I note I am the only non-academic on this panel, but am only a journalist, a mere sojourner in the epiphenomena of the everyday, but . . ." and he then proceeded to demolish the arguments of the three previous speakers. "A mere sojourner in the epiphenomena of the everyday," wonderful—Henry James, whom Hilton loved, çould not have topped it.

Hilton would not be long at the *New Leader.* He became art news editor at the *New York Times* in 1965 and would later, in 1974, become its major art critic. In 1980, when Aleksandr Solzhenitsyn arrived in this country, he would allow only Hilton to interview him for the *New York Times*, understanding that Hilton shared his, Solzhenitsyn's, love of truth and understanding of the toll that political and cultural nihilism took wherever it was permitted. I have always thought that a great tribute to Hilton's seriousness, integrity, honor.

I left the *New Leader* before Hilton. I attempted at first to find a better job in New York. Through the auspices of Joel Blocker, I had an interview at *Newsweek* with a senior editor there named Edwin Diamond. A miserable interview it turned out to be, during which Diamond, showing little interest in me, took no fewer than four phone calls while I sat on the other side of his desk. I had an interview for the job of associate editor at *Commentary* with Norman Podhoretz, who, during the interview, told me that anything good that appeared in the *New Leader* was there by mistake, and gave me an Irving Howe book, *A World More Attractive: A View of Modern Literature and Politics*, to review. The review never ran, and I was not offered the job. I next interviewed for an editor's job at the Chicago textbook firm of Scott Foresman, an interview that seemed to go extremely well, until three weeks after it I was informed that the company felt it too risky to pay the expense of bringing in people from outside Chicago.

After these disappointments, I decided I had to leave New York. Once my wife and I had won custody of her two older sons and the birth—by uninduced labor—of my own second son, I found myself, at the age of twenty-six, living with four children on a low salary in New York and getting any of my own writing done all but impossible. My wife and I decided to return to Little Rock. I sent her off with the four children, and not long after closed up our Flushing apartment. I followed roughly a month later on a Greyhound bus, the only detail of which long ride I recall was getting a shave from a barber at the stop in Memphis. I had not told anyone at the *New Leader* that I was leaving the magazine, and only did so, in a brief and rather curt note to Mike Kolatch, after I arrived, now unemployed, in Little Rock.

Chapter Ten

Poverty Warrior

In Little Rock, my wife had found a charming white house, up on a slight hill, with an ample front porch that had a wide swing. The house was originally built by the parents of the current occupant of the larger house next door, an older southern woman who in the early 1960s still referred to Blacks as "darkies." The rent was a reasonable $100 a month. The house was walking distance from downtown Little Rock.

The problem was I hadn't any clue about where to find a job. The *Arkansas Gazette*, onto hard times, was not hiring. I applied for work as a salesman at Pfeifer's and Cohn's, Little Rock's two large department stores, but heard nothing back. Four or five worrisome weeks passed. Then Dorothy Williams, my wife's sister, reported that a member of her Baptist church, a man named Olen Thomas, was the director of the North Little Rock Urban Renewal Agency and had a job opening. I arranged for an interview. Thomas was looking for, in effect, a public relations man, someone who could write public releases for his agency and oversee correspondence going out of the office. At the interview, he seemed, and later proved in fact to be, a good man, and at the interview's end he hired me for the job.

I was the only non-southerner in the office. For a time, I could fall back on that male lingua franca, sports, as a subject of conversation. My colleagues and I came from radically different worlds. One among them, a genial man named Harold Russell, was currently building his own house on weekends. When I happened to mention to him that I needed to replace something called a "throwout bearing" in my used Corvair—the car, by the way, featured for its flaws in Ralph Nader's book *Unsafe at Any Speed*—Harold told me that replacing it presented no real problem. "All you have to do is lift the engine and screw in the bearing underneath." Lift the engine? He told me that here all I needed was to get a #197 pulley, park the car between two strong trees, and with the aid of the pulley lift up the engine and screw in the bearing. Simple enough, no? Had I attempted it, I could imagine the next day's headline in the *Arkansas Gazette*: "Jewish Man Found Dead under Corvair Engine, Car Parked Between Two Trees in North Little Rock."

For a few years afterward, whenever I brought one of my cars in for repair, I would casually mention that I had just installed a throwout bearing in it, suggesting that I had done it myself and thus was not a man for any mechanic to attempt to cheat. Much later I learned that only cars with manual transmissions, or clutches, had throwout bearings. *Gotcha, Schmuckowitz!* these various mechanics must have thought.

My job at the North Little Rock Urban Renewal Agency was less than all-consuming, so in my ample spare time I decided to write an article for *Harper's* with the title "The Row Over Urban Renewal." Urban renewal at that time was an issue, which is to say very much in the flux of controversy. On the one hand, it was thought to comport with sensible planning; on the other, it was thought to upend minority groups and destroy the natural jumble that made city life so pleasing. In the intellectual realm, Lewis Mumford represented the former position, Jane Jacobs, with her book *The Death and Life of Great American Cities*, the latter.

Edited between 1935 and 1967 by a man named John Fischer, *Harper's* couldn't then have been more middlebrow in its point of view or general in its interests. The subtitles of so many of its articles ran roughly along the lines of "Quietly and unbeknownst to millions of Americans, there has been a revolution in . . . birdwatching, coal-mining, croquet, seal-hunting, cannabalism . . ." you fill in the subject. But the magazine had a wide readership and, as I was to discover, genuine influence.

My article, which set out the controversy over urban renewal while emphasizing its positive aspects, ran to roughly seven thousand words. My total knowledge of the subject ran to perhaps ten thousand words. As a result of the article's publication in *Harper's*, I became, for a period of roughly six months, one of the country's leading authorities on housing. I was offered a job as a speechwriter for Robert Weaver, secretary of the Department of Housing and Urban Development in Washington, and another on the planning commission of the city of Baltimore. I was invited to give speeches, appear on panels on the subjects of urban renewal and housing. I was, *mirabile dictu*, an expert, which has ever since caused me to distrust all experts.

On one of the panels on which I appeared, that at the University of Chicago Law School, I was seated next to a man named Julian Levi, who had engineered the vast urban renewal project in Hyde Park, the neighborhood surrounding the University of Chicago. When a young woman on the panel from New York University attacked urban renewal, Levi turned to me and, in a voice well above a whisper, said, "That whore doesn't know what she's talking about." I shook my head, smiled, wishing I were seated elsewhere. Years later, when I mentioned the name Julian Levi to Saul Bellow, he replied, "Ah, the great urban renewal man. They ought to devote a statue to him here in Hyde Park, then immediately blow it up."

Such advances as I have known in my life have come about owing to my writing. Not long after my *Harper's* article appeared, I was interviewed and then selected for the job of director of the anti-poverty program in Pulaski County, Arkansas. The man who interviewed me, Cal Ledbetter, had gone to Princeton and thence to the University of Arkansas School of Law, and was prominent in local Democratic politics. The anti-poverty program, better known as the "War on Poverty," was a key item in Lyndon Johnson's Great Society.

I believed less than wholeheartedly in a War on Poverty, or in a Great Society, let alone in that old rogue Lyndon Johnson. What I did believe in was the civil rights movement, with its devotion to wiping off the books the various cruel laws that still enforced segregation throughout the South along with some in the North and its goal of an integrated society. I also much admired the movement's leaders: Martin Luther King Jr., Whitney Young, A. Philip Randolph, Roy Wilkins, James Farmer, and Bayard Rustin. Had I not married so young and come to have a family of four children so quickly, I like to think that I would have taken an active hand in the civil rights movement, joining sit-ins and much else.

The anti-poverty program, I felt, gave me that chance, if only in an indirect way. As director of the program for Pulaski County, which encompassed both Little Rock and North Little Rock and their suburbs, I felt I could help advance the goals of the civil rights movement by teaching its local leaders how to tap into federal funds for the movement's ends. At the outset, there was a bureaucracy to deal with. I had to set up a board for the anti-poverty program. I was allowed to hire an assistant and two field-workers, as they were called, and a secretary. As an assistant, I hired an extraordinary woman named Ruth Arnold, white, in her forties, originally from Milwaukee, devoted to integration in the most serious way. Two young Black men were my field-workers, one of whom, Howard Love, went on to become the president of the Urban League of Arkansas.

My aim was to begin modestly, but on what I took to be firm grounds. The anti-poverty programs I chose to begin with in aiding the poor, who in Pulaski County were chiefly Blacks, were legal aid, family planning, and financial advisement. The most exotic-sounding items, such as care for children run by the elderly, I took a pass on. I also put out feelers to the local chapters of the Student Nonviolent Coordinating Committee (SNCC) and Congress of Racial Equality (CORE) to let them know that, working together, we might find ways to divert federal funds to their purposes.

I greatly admired those who worked in these civil rights groups, not least for their physical courage. They protested at a time when completely antipathetic southern sheriffs didn't mind siccing dogs on them and beating them up, both on the streets and in jail cells. Many of these civil rights workers were in their early twenties.

The local SNCC leader in Little Rock was Bill Hansen, white, young, and, arrested no fewer than forty-five times, a prisoner in several southern jails. In one, in Albany, Georgia, they crushed his jaw and broke several of his ribs. I remember taking him to lunch to explain ways that I might help SNCC with federal funds. I paid the modest check, and he insisted on leaving the tip.

"Oh, really!" I said jokingly. "Trotsky, you know, never tipped."

"Why not?" he asked.

"Because to tip is implicitly to support an unfair capitalist system."

"Really?" he said.

"Yep," I answered.

He picked his tip of three quarters off the table and returned them to his pocket.

As director of the anti-poverty program, I gave a number of talks about its programs in Black churches. Running twenty minutes or so, much of the content of these talks was taken from Michael Harrington's *The Other America: Poverty in the United States* (1962). The talks, filled with statistics, were rather dry. The only item I can remember from them was my recounting to my audiences that to this day there were children growing up in New York who had never seen, let alone eaten, an orange. Yet my dullish talks received what to me was an enthusiastic, though perhaps standard, Black evangelical response. "Tell it, brother," someone in one of my audiences might cry. Or: "Yeah, Jesus. Say it like it be!" I also recall a meeting with a number of leaders of the Little Rock Black community that I called to explain the anti-poverty program and at which the head of the Urban League began by saying:

"We're very informal here, Joe. But let me introduce you to our group." He then went round to name its members, every one of whom had a title: "President Green of Philander Smith College, Judge Perkins, Reverend Simms, Professor Tomkins, Police Captain Hodges . . ." I, it seems, was the only one in the room without a title.

As for the anti-poverty program itself, things did not go well. My first sense of its futility came when, in dealing with the central office in Washington, I was told that my request for funds of less than half a million dollars for programs would have to take a back seat to those programs, such as that in Houston, that ran to $10 million and more. Then the individual programs I had instituted seemed to backfire. My hope was that the legal aid under the anti-poverty program would be used to initiate legal actions against poor schooling, wretched public facilities for Blacks, and unfair voting practices. Instead, those who availed themselves of legal aid used it to sue one another: for divorce, collection of debts, small crimes. On the matter of birth control, one Black woman I spoke with on the subject closed off the discussion by saying, "Black man ain't gonna use no rubbers."

The crusher came with a phone call from a young woman, a graduate student at Columbia, working with the SNCC in Little Rock during the summer. A small number of New York graduate students came down to Little Rock every summer, some to work with the SNCC, some to teach in one of the city's two Black colleges, Philander Smith and Shorter. One of them told me that he was teaching the poetry of Paul Valéry, which must have caused both my eyebrows to shoot up. This young woman called to inform me that there was going to be a protest march on the state capitol building, and she thought I would want to march in it.

"I should much like to," I said, "but, given my job, it is important that I appear neutral, which makes it easier to help you people at SNCC."

"I don't see how marching in this protest ought to be a problem for you," she said.

"I'm afraid it would be a serious problem," I said.

"Maybe, then, you yourself are just part of the problem," she replied.

I had a two-word answer ready, but suppressed it.

"Thanks anyhow for letting me know about the march," I said, and hung up.

The persistence of poverty, I began to feel, was in part a political and certainly an economic problem, but perhaps just as much, if not more deeply, a cultural one. Programs, anti-poverty and others, might offer ameliorations but no true solutions. In fact, politics might just work against such solutions.

Around this time Stokely Carmichael, one of the young leaders of the SNCC, gave his "Black Power" speech. In that speech he called for Black people to unite, to recognize their heritage, to build a sense of community. The speech was a call for Black people to define their own goals, above all to lead their own organizations. Under the banner of Black Power, Carmichael was also calling for an end to integration as the chief goal of the civil rights movement. Around this time, Bill Hansen was asked to step down as head of the Little Rock SNCC chapter. My own thought as director of an anti-poverty program was to raise Blacks—or Negroes, as they then were called—into the middle class. Stokely Carmichael held that the middle class wasn't worth being integrated into. Two years later, Martin Luther

King Jr. was murdered, and with his death the appeal to conscience in the civil rights movement was replaced by the demand to own up to guilt, the proud dignity of a people who had suffered and persisted by an insistence on an angry and immitigable victim status.

Time, it seemed, for me to check out. But where to go? I hadn't any notion, until one day at lunch Jerry Neil introduced me to Harry Ashmore, who had left the *Arkansas Gazette* in 1959, first to work for Robert Hutchins at the Center for the Study of Democratic Institutions and then to become for three years the editor in chief of the *Encyclopaedia Britannica.* Ashmore was in Little Rock on a brief visit. When I met him, his official title at Britannica, Inc. was director of editorial research. We seemed to hit it off, and when I mentioned that I would soon be leaving the anti-poverty program, he suggested that I might be interested in a job at Britannica. The *Encyclopaedia* was planning an extensive revision, he told me, and he would be pleased to arrange an interview for me with its current editor, a man named Warren Preece.

The interview took place in New York. As luck would have it, I had published a book review the Sunday before in the *New York Times Book Review*, which in Warren Preece's mind apparently established my bona fides. (Through these years I had continued to review books for the *New Republic*, *Commentary*, and elsewhere.) The interview itself was not long—perhaps half an hour—and at its end I was offered the job of senior editor, at a salary of $18,000, nearly double what I was earning as director of the Pulaski County anti-poverty program. The job provided the extra bonus of my returning to Chicago, where Britannica, Inc.'s offices were. I left the interview feeling I had pulled off a successful bank job. The celebratory touchdown dance had not yet been invented, else I would have done one while awaiting the arrival of the elevator.

Chapter Eleven

EB

Encyclopaedia Britannica, Inc. was installed in Chicago on two ample floors in the Mandel-Lear warehouse, just east of the Gothic *Chicago Tribune* building. One floor was given over to its editorial and art departments, the other to its business and sales departments. Founded in Scotland in 1768, the *Encyclopaedia Britannica* had a nearly two-hundred-year history, acquiring along the way such impressive contributors as Albert Einstein, Sigmund Freud, Leon Trotsky, Benjamin Franklin, William Hazlitt, Alfred North Whitehead, Marie Curie, George Bernard Shaw, and Helen Wills. Stately in its many volumes, reliable in its factual material, in all respects authoritative, *Britannica* was easily the leading such reference work in the Anglophone, if not the entire, world.

When I arrived there in 1967, it was run by a hundred or so anonymous members of its editorial and art departments, the former whose job it was to add new and update old articles, the latter to supply photographs and maps to accompany these articles. Unknown soldiers all, they worked sedulously, and for less than grand salaries.

Although I did not know it at the time, I had been hired to undo their work. As *Britannica* neared its two hundredth anniversary, the feeling was that the time had come for a major revision. What form this revision ought to take had not been decided. I among others was hired to decide. Given that there was no encylopedia in the household in which I grew up, nor did I own an encyclopedia in my adult life, nor ever gave the matter of encyclopedias the least thought, this was, for me at least, rather a tall order.

One senior editor before me had been hired, a man six or seven years older than I named Robert Hazo. Robert's family was Lebanese, Maronite Christian. He had gone to St. John's College in Annapolis, the decisive event in his life—as it was in that of everyone who went to this great books school. Before *Britannica*, he had worked for Mortimer Adler, when his office, modestly known as the Institute for Philosophical Research, was in San Francisco. Robert had written a book, *The Idea of Love*, on one of Adler's 102 "Great Ideas." An unembarrassed elitist, Robert would on occasion refer to the editors working on *Britannica* as "Aristotle's natural slaves." Since initially there wasn't much work for either of us to do, we spent long hours smoking and schmoozing in one or the other of our offices, about politics, books, and our fellow employees.

Tall and dark, Robert was a professional smoker. When he wasn't smoking a small Schimmelpenninck cigar, he had one of his many Dunhill pipes going. He spent a fair amount of time at Dunhill's, which was only a few blocks from Britannica's offices. He told the story of a fire alarm going off one night in the Mies van der Rohe apartment building on Lake Shore Drive where he lived, which caused every occupant to emerge from their apartments with their valuables: important documents, paintings, jewelry. Robert told me, with a smile denoting the triviality of his choice, that what he brought out of his apartment that evening was his rack of Dunhill pipes.

Robert had studied as a graduate student at Princeton and in Paris, where he encountered Allan Bloom, who once told me that he was envious of Robert's winning all the attractive younger women. (Allan in those days was still covering up his own homosexuality.) Robert once recounted the story of the landlady from whom he rented a room in Princeton having caught him with a girl, which was against the house rules. "I am shocked at you, Mr. Hazo," she exclaimed. "I took you for a nice young man, clean and cut from the Ivory League."

While interested in women, Robert was one of nature's bachelors. He never dated anyone who lived beyond walking distance of his own apartment. "The screwing I get," he once told me, "isn't worth the screwing I get." He was always well turned out, wearing one or another of his expensive gray or black suits and somber neckties. I've read that the least marriageable man is the fifty-year-old bachelor who has never married—least marriageable because too highly critical. Here Robert qualified. He died, back in his hometown of Pittsburgh after he had left *Britannica*, where he ran a great books seminar of sorts for adults at the University of Pittsburgh, of a heart attack at the age of seventy-four.

Robert kept his life as simple as possible. He once came into my office with a worried look. When I asked him what was wrong, he said that his nephew Sam might need an operation four or five years from now. I was myself at the time going through a divorce, trying to sell a house, struggling to keep a family of four kids afloat. I congratulated myself in restraining from saying, "A possible operation of a nephew four or five years from now, no wonder you're worried. That's serious!"

Our assignment was to find a possible theme for what was to be the new *Britannica.* I decided on the theme of struggle. Life begins with the struggle of childbirth, nations struggle to come into existence, creation of all kinds entails struggle. I was asked to write a paper defending the theme. A useless exercise, really, for an encyclopedia, by definition, is an encirclement of all knowledge, and no single theme can hope to cover so wide a span. Nevertheless I wrote a paper on struggle, and today can only say that I am glad it is lost and hope it never turns up.

Work at Britannica was easy enough. Weeks would go by with our having little or nothing to do. Soon a new editorial arrangement was established that called for a breakdown of the content of the *Britannica* into ten parts with a senior editor hired for each of the various parts: (1) physics, chemistry, and astronomy; (2) geology, geography, oceanography; (3) taxonomy, molecular and cell biology, physiology, neuroscience, ecology; (4) human evolution, medicine, psychology; (5) politics, economics, education, and law; (6) the arts; (7) the history of technology and the different technologies; (8) religion; (9) history organized by continent and epoch; and (10) the branches of knowledge: mathematics, logic, science, philosophy, humanities, library science.

New editors were hired. Some were failed academics; a few former journalists. I recall walking with Robert Hazo on our way to lunch behind three of the arts editors, and his remarking, "Ah, look at them, enjoying their turgid little ironies."

One interesting figure among the editors assigned to work on the revision of *Britannica*, hired on loan from Mortimer Adler's office, was Charles Van Doren, the son of the Columbia University teacher and poet Mark Van Doren. Charles was of course famous for his appearance on the television quiz show *Twenty-One*, where he won $129,000 (the equivalent of $1,244,605 in current dollars). He was on the cover of *Time* on February 11, 1957—Leonard Bernstein was on the cover the week before and Martin Luther King Jr. the week after—and for a brief stretch may have been the most famous man in America. When Charles confessed at a congressional hearing in 1959 that he had been fed the answers to the questions he was asked on the show, he soon turned into the most infamous man in the country. The first lunch I went to with Charles I happened to mention that I was, later that day, closing on a house I had bought. "Ah," he said, "the last time I closed on a house, in New York, I had two jobs, one at NBC and one at Columbia, and the very next day I had neither." This was his way of clearing the air on his scandal. One never wanted to get into an argument with Charles, for the sad and simple reason one had too natural an advantage over him, a nationally renowned bullshitter. Growing up in the Van Doren family, Charles had wide learning, but its depth remained a puzzle, at least to me. He seemed to know a lot, but believe in little. Had his scandal not been revealed, Charles, who was enamored of the 1960s, might have gone into politics, probably as a progressive *avant la lettre*.

That Charlie (as I came to know him) found a job with Mortimer Adler after his scandal broke is testimony to the strength of what I came to think the Columbia network, or intellectual mafia. Mark Van Doren, Jacques Barzun, Clifton Fadiman, Joseph Wood Krutch, and

Mortimer Adler fed each other work over the years. In 1943, when Robert Wood, chairman of Sears, Roebuck and Co., divested his company of some among its many holdings, he donated the *Encylopaedia Britannica* to the University of Chicago. Robert Hutchins, then president of the university, in turn passed it along to his vice president for public relations, the former advertising man William Benton (of Benton & Bowles), for a minimal sum, with the arrangement that Benton would return a royalty on all sets sold to the University of Chicago.

Hutchins would later bring on Mortimer Adler, who brought along his Columbia compatriots Mark Van Doren, Jacques Barzun, and Clifton Fadiman to work on *Britannica*. Clifton (or Kip, as he was known) Fadiman's story was that he had hoped to go to graduate school in English at Columbia, but was told that the English department there already had accepted Mr. Lionel Trilling, its way of saying that the graduate student quota for Jews was filled, thank you very much. The story, told by Fadiman, was that, denied the chance of a life of scholarship, he went for money, and a fairly powerful moneymaker he turned out to be. He had earlier achieved fame as the host of a much-listened-to radio show called *Information Please* that ran from 1938 to 1951, he helped found the Book of the Month Club and stayed on as one of its panel of judges, and he worked as a consultant on *Britannica* for the impressive (for that day) annual salary of $63,000. Earlier he had been one of the main book reviewers for the *New Yorker.*

Kip Fadiman had a Jewish problem, and not only with the Columbia English department. Born in Brooklyn in 1904, the son of a druggist and a nurse, he expressed his discomfort with his Jewishness through the novel mode of extreme pretension. At a meeting about the reorganization of *Britannica*, he composed a rubric for the new table of contents that ran: "The beginning of cinema: the curious confluence of an emerging technology and a surgent entrepreneurial ethnic group." When this was read aloud in one of our many editorial meetings, Robert Hazo passed a note to me that read "I think he means the Jews got there first."

I once heard Kip say, "What's left for me: a few wines, certain cheeses." He was sixty-three at the time. His daughter Anne wrote a book called *The Wine-Lover's Daughter*, about the inordinate importance he placed on fine wine. Fran Lebowitz has said that there are three kinds of people: ordinary people who talk about other people and current events; highly cerebral people who talk about ideas; and stupid people who talk about wine.

I was put in charge of a stable of eight or nine writers, a few hired by Warren Preece, the rest by me. Among them were a poet who had previously worked at *Time* named Mark Perlberg; Ralph Tyler Jr., whose father worked at the Center for Advanced Study in the Behavioral Sciences in Palo Alto; a young Black novelist named Ron Fair, whom when I hired I asked what he was expecting in the way of a salary, to which he casually answered, "Eleven, twelve thousand." I offered him $13,000, when I could have paid him as much as $18,000, and felt guilty ever after.

I was also able to hire Peter Jacobsohn, an old acquaintance from the *New Leader* days. Peter was perhaps twenty years older than I. He was the business manager at the magazine and handled its paucity of ads. He had gone from the *New Leader* to the publishing firm of W. W. Norton, from which he had recently been laid off. Peter was the son of Siegfried Jacobsohn, a theater critic and editor of *Die Weltbühne*, or *The World Stage*, an important cultural magazine during the Weimar era in which he praised the work of Bertolt Brecht, Hugo von Hofmannsthal, Arthur Schnitzler, and others, and whose last issue was published in 1933, when it was banned by the Nazis. Siegfried Jacobsohn died in his mid-forties.

With the rise of Hitler, Peter and his mother immigrated to England. When the war broke out, Peter, interned by the British, was sent off to Australia, where his chief memory was of rolling out and marking off the lines on clay tennis courts. Peter, who spoke with a slight German accent, never became entirely acclimated to America, even after decades of living here. I remember him asking me, during the *New Leader* days, how much a baby costs, for his wife, Annette, also a German émigré, was pregnant with what would be their only child, a son, Nicholas. I cited the bill charged by my wife's physician and by the hospital for her stay there during her delivery of our second son. "No, no, no," Peter said. "I mean, how much is it likely to cost for the life of the thing."

To Peter, at Britannica, I was always "the colonel." Our understanding, never spoken of directly, was that I was to protect him on the job, which I was pleased to do. At one point I wrote a review of Peter Gay's *Weimar Culture* for the *New Republic* under his name. One wanted to do things for Peter. He had charm, but of an unusual kind: people wanted him to like them. This, I thought, was owing to his immitigable Europeanness. These were still the years when in America true culture was viewed as European culture, and to be liked by Peter Jacobsohn was, in effect, to have been approved by Europe. Not that Peter was in any way cruel or harsh in his judgments, for he had no side to him whatsoever.

After Peter departed Britannica, Inc., he moved to Boston. He had always been lucky in real estate, buying homes—in Dobbs Ferry, New York; Highland Park, Illinois; Wayland, Massachusetts—low and selling them high, and thereby, along with his doing some freelance editing, he was able to live out his days without great financial worry. Peter died in his early eighties. I prefer to think that God, too, wanted Peter to like him, and therefore arranged a most comfortable accommodation for him in heaven that he acquired at well below market price.

Britannica had a small number of interesting characters walking its halls. A Greek named Alexis Lladdas, who bore the title "vice president international," was said to have faced and somehow survived a Nazi firing squad in Greece. In his mid-fifties, he was married to a woman in her twenties, and had a mistress in her mid-fifties. When asked to explain this strange reversal of the standard procedure—older wife, younger mistress—he claimed that, with a wife only in her mid-twenties, he needed someone to talk to.

Another impressive character at Britannica was a man roughly my age named Martin Self. Martin was a New Yorker, a lawyer by education, though one who failed to pass the bar and never retook it. On *Britannica* he worked on legal articles, though not all that efficiently. He was smart, subtle, in every way an original. He dressed like a European, but of no known country. He made a meal of the lung-ripping Gauloises cigarettes he smoked. He kept his own hours, coming in late, staying after hours. Martin had gone to Bard College, where his mentor was Heinrich Blücher, the husband of Hannah Arendt. He once told Blücher that he was going to take his life because he could think of no reason to go on living. "Don't take your life," Herr Blücher told him, "we'll find you a reason."

Martin took especial pleasure in taking the measure of others. He once referred to a member of the editorial staff as a communist. I told him I thought this was nonsense, the man was no communist. "You don't understand," he replied, "if it were the 1930s and the American Communist Party still throve, he would have been in it." He, Martin, had an impressive detachment. If he had a politics, I was never able to determine what they might be. My best guess is that he thought the most interesting things in life were above and beyond politics, which is of course true. During those days, when anti-Vietnam War protests were rife, a young woman in the office wearing a protester's black armband, asked Martin if he were going to that afternoon's protest march. "No, Naomi," he said, "afternoons such as this I generally spend at the graveside of George Santayana."

Like no one else I have ever known, Martin, in manner and in cast of mind, fit in nowhere. He didn't last long at Britannica, for one early evening, after everyone had apparently gone home, he decided to inspect the contents of the editor in chief's desk drawers and filing cabinets, and was caught at it by his secretary, who, unbeknownst to him, had also stayed late. He likely did so as much out of curiosity as out of any personal motive. The editor in chief fired him the next day.

Not long after, Martin landed a job working for Elsevier, the European reference-book firm, which sent him off to London. Martin once referred to himself to me as a "permanent transient," and London, an international city, seemed a more fitting location for him than Chicago. He had earlier married a Dutch woman named Anka, and in London they had a child, a son, Gabriel. We stayed in touch. I spent time with him on two different visits I made to England. He called me on the few occasions that he returned to the United States, where he had a younger brother and older sister. On his last call he told me that he had cancer, of the brain. He was in his mid-forties. He died from his brain tumors and in his last months suffered from aphasia. I miss him still. Martin was an original, and how many thoroughly original people does one encounter in a lifetime?

In 1968, in a surprise move—surprising to those of us who worked there—Warren Preece was removed as editor in chief of *Britannica* and replaced by Sir William Haley. Then sixty-seven, Sir William had been director of the *Manchester Guardian*, director general of the BBC, and then editor of the London *Times*. Only the job of editor of the *Oxford English Dictionary* was missing to make his résumé perfect. Sir William was hired by William Benton, doubtless to commemorate the two hundredth anniversary of the encyclopedia, which was celebrated in England, by having a superior Englishman at its helm. Benton, a coarse man, who claimed a close relation with Adlai Stevenson and Hubert Humphrey, longed for distinction, and William Haley was hired to bring it.

Along with his editorial and broadcasting jobs, Sir William had published a collection of essays, *Talking of Books*, under the name of Oliver Edwards. He was part of the intellectual aristocracy of English life of that day, an aristocracy that included such figures as H. R. Trevor-Roper, Isaiah Berlin, Anthony Quinton, Gilbert Ryle, D. S. Carne-Ross, Michael Oakeshott, Hugh Lloyd-Jones, John Sparrow, and others. It is an intellectual aristocracy that seems to have disappeared in our day, leaving those doleful knights Sir Mick Jagger and Sir Elton John as representative Englishmen in a country sadly losing its intellectual distinction.

Sir William was taciturn, but one straightaway sensed his gravity.

Here was a man I could much admire, and I could easily imagine working with him for a decade or however long it took to revise the *Encyclopaedia Britannica* under his stewardship. At one of the rare editorial meetings he called, he asked one of the arts editors, a man named Robert Loescher, to describe what he thought might be a fit form for a biographical article in *Britannica* on a visual artist. Loescher set out his description of his notion of such an article, feeling no need to go into intricate detail and instead ending several of his sentences with "blah, blah, blah." After the meeting, Sir William called me into his office. "Mr. Epstein," he said, "we must see to it that nothing Mr. Loescher writes goes out of this office without our first checking it."

The hiring of Sir William interrupted the work on the great revision of *Britannica.* The engineer of that revision was Mortimer Adler. An indexer in philosopher's clothes, Adler in his *Syntopicon* had produced two volumes with roughly 163,000 references to the 32,000 pages of the *Great Books of the Western World*, also published by Britannica. Reviewing this vast work in the *New Yorker,* Dwight Macdonald in a strong attack referred to it as "the Book of the Millennium Club." Mortimer believed that everyone was educable, and that the study of the great books was the first step to becoming educated; he felt that these books, soon to be supplemented by an *Encyclopaedia Britannica* of his design, would complete the job of providing all the world with the means to an education. Mortimer's intentions were of the highest; his grasp of reality of the lowest.

Mortimer was high on the past century's list of savant idiots, or intellectually dazzling figures who get all important things wrong. I came to view him as an essentially comic character. Endless are the anecdotes about his misperceptions. At one point he was courting a woman to whom he attempted to write love poems. Writing on a yellow legal pad, he tore up page after page. When he went off to lunch, his curious secretary entered his office and found, atop a fresh page, the single word "Whereas." A pity Aristophanes had died millennia before, for he would have found a rich subject in Mortimer.

Mortimer favored a Rube Goldberg sort of encyclopedia, divided into three main parts. One part devoted to longish articles on grand subjects to be known as the Macropaedia; one given over to brief articles on merely factual subjects to be known as the Micropaedia; and, finally, a vast combined table of contents and index for which he invented the neologism Propaedia. He began with the novel notion of creating an index, which he referred to as "the table of intents," before supplying the actual content.

Sir William was not in the least interested in Mortimer Adler's notions of how *Britannica* might be revised. His own, simpler program was to improve the contents of the set by bringing in the most brilliant contributors he could find, but generally to leave it stand in its present simple alphabetical organization and format. I was myself wholeheartedly a Haley man. I gave him a copy of Dwight Macdonald's book *Against the American Grain*, which contained his essay on Adler's edition of *Great Books of the Western World* and which he returned to me with a single word, "Devastating." No two men were more unalike: Sir William, modest, suave, intellectually sophisticated; Mortimer, vain, coarse, intellectually crude. They presented a genuine choice, a choice the outcome of which put the destiny of the great *Encyclopaedia Britannica* at stake.

The decision—Adler or Haley?—was ultimately in the hands of Robert Hutchins. William Benton entrusted most intellectual matters to Hutchins, especially those having to do with the *Encylopaedia Britannica*, which, after all, Hutchins had originally bestowed upon him. A great man in some ways, one of Robert Hutchins's failings was his tendency to be loyal to the wrong people, Mortimer Adler among them. My friend Edward Shils remarked about this friendship that "at least Prince Hal had the good sense, once he became king, to get rid of Falstaff." Doubtless out of loyalty to Adler, Hutchins favored his plan for the new *Britannica* over Sir William Haley's, which forced Haley, scarcely more than a year on the job, to depart the editorship and return to his home in the Channel Islands. Staying on under Adler was not my notion of how I wished to spend my life. When I, not too long after, left Britannica, Sir William, with whom I had begun to correspond, wrote to me: "I am glad that you have left the Britannica. The people there worship different gods than we."

After the fifteenth, or the Mortimer Adler, edition of *Britannica* was published, readers began to complain about the want of a traditional index, finding that his Propaedia didn't do the job, and two traditional index volumes had to be added. Later, Bill Gates proposed to take *Britannica* online, but the then president of the company, an Englishman named Peter Norton, himself a salesman, saw little point in Gates's proposal, feeling that door-to-door sales was the only road to the company's continued success. A fatal decision, as it turned out.

The last printed edition of the *Encyclopaedia Britannica* came out in 2010. It is still in business online, but a shadow of its old self, its prestige and authority leeched away. The once grand *Encyclopaedia Britannica* is gone.

Chapter Twelve

Downward Heights

After my divorce, I cannot say I played the field. I didn't have a date for more than a year. As the father of four sons—ages fourteen, twelve, eight, and six—I scarcely qualified as an eligible bachelor. I divided my time between my work and raising these children, without any left over for that playful field.

About love at first sight I do not know, but I do know that I was immediately struck at my first sight of my second wife. I was talking with Robert Hazo and another *Britannica* editor when I noted her walking toward us down a long aisle at the EB offices. She was slender, smallish, with an intelligent face of perfect symmetry. I asked who she was and was told her name was Barbara Maher and that she worked in the art department. I later learned that she was responsible for placing and replacing the photographs in the encyclopedia, a job requiring a combination of meticulous attention to detail with a sound aesthetic sense.

We eventually met in the course of our work. At our first meeting, in my office, I suggested two paper cups of tea, and hence a tea party. She had high cheekbones, an easy, lovely, slightly shy smile, and to my eye resembled a combination of the young Audrey Hepburn and Jean Simmons. She also had a natural refinement, both in dress and manner. She turned out to be the least vulgar person I have ever known, with a kind and generous heart, the highest qualification above all others to be found in anyone.

In 1969, when first we met, she was thirty-four, a year older than I. She had grown up in the northwest Chicago suburb of Arlington Heights, was salutatorian of her high school class there, and later a Phi Beta Kappa at DePauw University in Indiana. Her father was vice president for advertising at the Florsheim Shoe Company. She was a reader of E. M. Forster, Anthony Trollope, Thucydides, and Henry James. We shared a love for the music of Mozart and the ballets of Balanchine.

We talked a fair amount about the movies, and I suggested we one day take off from work to see a movie together. We did one Friday afternoon; the movie, playing in the Loop, was *Midnight Cowboy.* Roughly halfway through I reached out to hold her hand. She later told me she thought it rather bold of me. We parted at the end of the movie, she for her apartment in Evanston, me to make dinner for my four sons in the western suburb of Berwyn. It was, I guess, a date of sorts.

The first time we did go out on an official date, I chose a restaurant on the far South Side of Chicago called the Tropical Hut, which specialized in barbecued ribs. Why a rib joint, I do not know. We both ordered calf's liver, lest, wearing bibs, munching away on rib bones, we each appeared inelegant to the other. This soon become a joke between us.

We shared many jokes. She seemed to enjoy my humor, much of which played off the endless peculiarities of language. When, after a long day's work, her eyelids tended to flutter to a close, I said that she had "the G. Gordon Liddies," after the name of one of the so-called plumbers in the Watergate affair that brought down Richard Nixon. Making meat sauce I put a spoon of sugar into the pot, and asked her what movie my doing so reminded her of: "*Absorba the Grease*, with Anthony Quinn," I said. I was always pleased to evoke that smile, to make her laugh. Once, in London together, sitting at a common table at a coffee shop in Marylebone, a man asked if we were brother and sister. I felt a high compliment in the question.

In Barbara, I found my life's companion. She was someone whose fidelity I could count on. I never tired of gazing at her face. I was pleased that she rapidly won the affection of my mother, not an easy critic. Being chosen for her partner elevated me in my own eyes. "I knew I could trust you," she said to me when once I asked her whatever she saw in me. Trust never to hurt, humiliate, let down the other is at the heart of any serious relationship.

We hung out together for nearly seven years before we married. The reason was the chaos of my own domestic life, what with four boys to raise and a freelance (one of the world's great misnomers) writing life to conduct. Barbara had not been married before and was not eager to have children; nor was I ready for more. By the time we did marry, in 1976, after the two older boys, my stepsons, were off to college, she was forty and it was in any case dangerously late to have children even if we had wanted them.

Before my second marriage, I was living at the time with my four sons in a six-flat building that I called, if only to myself, Downward Heights. (The building was in Evanston, where Barbara lived.) Downward because, with only one exception, every apartment in the building was occupied by people who had seen better days. On the third floor, next to me and my young male brood, lived the Runyons, both married before. Byrnie (after her maiden name of Byrnes) Runyon was an attractive redhead, with two redheaded sons, Patrick and Billy, from her first marriage. Paul Runyon, who worked in advertising sales, had a son living in California, with whom he had lost touch. Paul and Byrnie had a daughter, Amy, beautiful and vulnerable, who in her early twenties would OD on drugs. On the second floor lived Mrs. Armstrong, a drinking woman, who had a son with severe learning disabilities. On the first floor was Citta Erie, with two young children, a boy and a girl, no husband, and an impressively potty mouth; her money came from her deceased father's medical patents. Across from Citta lived the Lowmans, George and Judy, with a young son; Judy's father was big in railroads, and frequently sent his chauffeur round to pick them up. The youngest couple in the building, they hadn't yet time to fall downward. I recall their three-year-old son one day making his way up to the third floor, and Paul Runyon saying to him, "Jonathan, come up any farther and I'll cut your little pecker off." As the boy turned back, Paul said to me, "That ought to give him something to tell his psychoanalyst in later years." No, Barbara wouldn't have fit in at Downward Heights.

With my two stepsons off to college, I and my younger sons departed Downward Heights for the more normally occupied six-flat building one door to the south. Barbara and I were married, by a judge in Skokie, with her brother, then a physicist at Bell Labs in New Jersey, and one of her friends as witnesses, on a warm day in February. Down now to two sons and with a new and more orderly apartment, I was a newly married man. A biographical note accompanying an article I had written in *Chicago* magazine appeared not long after that read "Joseph Epstein lives in Evanston with his second wife." Barbara asked if in the future I could arrange that editors could change that to read "with his final wife." Now that we have been married for forty-seven years, I believe that the change she requested is in order.

An instance of the decline of the extended family is the case of my own stepsons, Lynn and David. Lynn married young, though he would have no children, became a computer programmer, departed for the Northwest, and has lived out his days in the state of Washington. David followed his mother to Las Vegas, married twice, and spent his working life there with Bally's, the casino firm. Apart from a rare phone call, and an occasional email, I have all but lost touch with both and have seen neither for decades. I like to think the good feeling we share among us has not lessened, but neither has it prompted meetings or more regular contact. Sad.

As for my two sons, the older, Mark, seemed from an early age to be on his own. He did well in school, he found various hobbies, he hired on at the age of thirteen to work at a nearby Junior League vintage clothing store. One day, I upbraided him for playing rock music loudly in his room, asking, "How can you study with the music turned up so high?" He answered: "I'm getting all A's, Dad. Are you sure you want me to turn the music down?"

At Evanston Township High School, he was editor of the *Evanstonian*, the school paper. As editor, he spoke at his graduation, strongly criticizing the administration of the school, which was not at all what was expected of a graduation speech. I was proud of his courage in saying what he thought it necessary to say. I don't recall his ever asking me for help with any of his schoolwork, or really for much else apart from his food, shelter, and fees for his education, for none of which he had to ask.

"The one useful thing you told me, Dad," he said to me later in life, "is to try to get into what the world thinks is a good university. You said I'd find that it isn't as good as all that, but at least I won't spend the rest of my life thinking how much better my life would be if only I had gone to a good university." He never asked my advice about what schools to apply to; he didn't need it. Nor did we go on a tour of schools, as many kids nowadays do with their parents. After he had sent off his applications, he received notice that he was on the waiting list at Harvard, was turned down at the University of Virginia, accepted at the University of Chicago (where he didn't really want to go), and accepted at the University of Michigan. "If I have to go to the University of Michigan," he said to me, "my life is essentially over." I told him that if he truly believed that, I wasn't going to pay for his going there. But the story has a happy ending: he was shortly after accepted by Stanford, which he attended.

At Stanford, Mark ended up one of the school's student body presidents. From this position he did what he could to make life miserable for Donald Kennedy, then the school's president and a noted appeaser on all significant subjects, not least the early de-Westernizing of the curriculum in the name of political correctness. After graduation, Mark took a job with Smith Barney in its San Francisco office. After a few years there he went into a partnership with a man named Michael Ogden, acquiring bonds and doing the financing for smaller towns and school districts. He soon became a serious money earner. He married at thirty-six and had two children, a boy and a girl. A good son, though he stayed on the West Coast, he bought an apartment in Evanston, which he visited two or three times a year, allowing me to spend time with him and my grandchildren. His mind, I had long before realized, was more capacious than mine, he had a higher threshold for dealing with chaos, and was in most ways more intelligent than I. "When a son becomes a man," an Arab proverb has it, "make him your brother." I did so with Mark, though today it is far from clear which of us is the older brother.

Things did not go so smoothly with Burton, Mark's eighteen-months-younger brother. He was born a chubby child, a little Buddha, who early took on the nickname Jibby, which he was called and smiled at hearing when tickled. His mother, my first wife, made no bones about making it clear that he, Burt, was her favorite child. Charming as a boy, as he grew older, his charm increased. Once, when he was perhaps five years old, walking along the lakefront in Evanston, he stopped before two men who were fishing off an embankment. He asked permission to stay with them for a bit. I agreed, and when I came back from my brief errand, he was holding a fishing pole, having charmed one of the men into letting him fish. He was a natural salesman.

Earlier, when Burt was just three years old, while we were living in Little Rock, one of his half brothers, quite by mistake, pushed a safety scissors into his left eye, causing him to lose the eye. He wore a false eye for the rest of his life. One cannot know for certain, but the loss of his eye may have made him wilder than normal, as if to prove that his injury didn't in any way incapacitate him. He wasn't the good student his brother was. More like his father, me, he was bored by school and didn't much mind showing it. Oddly, I one day discovered him reading, on his own initiative, *War and Peace*, though we never spoke about it. Senior year he dropped out of Evanston Township High, and I had to enroll him in a YMCA school in order for him to get his high school diploma.

Not long after, Burt moved to Las Vegas to be with his mother and her fifth husband, Monte Shields. Monte now worked for one of the Vegas casinos and got Burt a job there. Burt somehow screwed it up and was fired. Monte and his mother decided not to let him laze round the house unemployed, and insisted he depart the premises at nine in the morning out into the Nevada heat and not return until the normal working day was done. I don't know how long this went on, but at one point Burt called to ask if I thought I could get him into a college.

Drake University in Des Moines was the school I helped him apply to, and, owing to his high scores on the ACT exam, he was accepted. I drove him there to help settle him in. He joined a fraternity at Drake, did well in school—well enough to want to transfer, which he did after his first year. He applied to the University of Massachusetts at Amherst, and again was accepted. Majoring in history, he graduated, and seemed well on his way to a normal career and life. But, then, it soon became clear, little about his life was to be normal.

After graduating, Burt returned to Chicago. His first job was selling real estate in North Chicago and Skokie for a firm run by a Chinese woman. He had succeeded at the job, but was turned down when he suggested she make him a partner. He apparently decided he didn't want to work for anyone else. He had $30,000 in Israeli bonds given to him by his grandfather that had become due, and he cashed them in and with the money bought two used limousines and went into the livery business. For a while he did well, but he was considered an interloper in the business by rivaling livery firms, a driver he had hired crashed one of the limos, and his success was only temporary. He sold the limos at a loss and went to work for a Greek family in the catering business.

He had in the meanwhile bought a condo on Sheridan Road. One night, when he was gone, his girlfriend—he seems never to have had trouble attracting women—a pretty young mathematician named Paula Black, jumped from his ninth-floor apartment to her death. He came to me, utterly shaken, and slept that night in the spare room in our apartment. Paula, I later learned, was a serious depressive.

Soon after, Burt abandoned his condo, and under the assumed name of James Baker—assumed because he didn't want his landlord to know that he had abandoned his condo—he rented an apartment in Hyde Park on Chicago's South Side. In Hyde Park he began an affair with an African American woman, who had two children of her own. Soon she turned up pregnant with his child. I remember being saddened by this news, feeling that the world didn't need more children born out of wedlock. After the child, a girl, was born, I didn't ask to see her or to have anything to do with her. I continued to see Burt, chiefly at family dinners at my parents' apartment, but this child of his was not a subject up for discussion.

I saw him intermittently. Once he drove up to show me a Chrysler convertible with Polo tan leather seats he was thinking of buying and asked my opinion about his doing so. Another time, at dinner at my parents', we discovered that we had each recently bought Movado wristwatches, his more elegant and doubtless more expensive than mine. He insisted we switch and, now, more than thirty years later, I still wear his watch, a reminder of his generous gesture.

Then one afternoon, around 4:00 p.m.—April 30, 1990—I had a call from the father of a friend of his, telling me, without much in the way of preamble, that my son Burt was dead, apparently of an overdose of drugs, in his Hyde Park apartment. I was not entirely surprised that he was using drugs. I did not cry or otherwise break down at the news. His death did not shock me, but left me stunned, without anything consolatory or even sensible to say. He was not yet twenty-eight. *What a waste!* was all I could think. *What a damn sad waste!* I still feel that.

In the same numb state of mind, I identified his body in one of the city's morgues and was presented with a death certificate that stated cause of death "opioid overdose." His burial, in our family plot in the Woodlawn Cemetery west of Chicago, is even more of a blur to me. All I can recall about it is my mother, who sensed her own approaching death from liver cancer, saying, as her grandson's body was being lowered into the ground, "I'll be with you soon, Jibby."

Only in recent years have I been able to think in a concentrated way about Burt's death. I think of all he missed in dying so young. I, of course, wonder how he would have turned out. After his death, I heard stories of his looking for fights in bars and other wildness. Would he have found work that satisfied him? Would he have been a good father? All questions with no answers.

One of the leading clichés of our day is "coming to closure." Come to Closure—it sounds to me more like an advertisement for a spa than a panacea for unremitting sadness. With the death of a child, I believe one never "comes to closure." Instead, one perennially feels something missing in one's life. Life goes on, of course, but with a permanent hole in it.

Burt's child, a daughter whose name is Annabelle and who has no memories of him, his having died when she was less than a year old, has told me that, in some ways, never having known her father is perhaps easier than having lost a father one has known and loved. She, as it turns out, is a remarkable person, beautiful, intelligent, gifted in all visual arts. Writing is a trade one learns in time; visual art and music appear to be inherent, gifts from God. From the age of three, Annabelle could draw well, knew colors, had a strong sense of visual composition.

Such are the oddities of life, my disappointment in my son Burt's having brought a child into the world happens to have been his (and, of course, her mother's) greatest gift to me. Annabelle was an irresistible child. One day, perhaps three years old, she was sitting on my lap as we watched on television an animated film about a fox who is ejected and sent out into the world from the house of human beings where he had been a pet. "Isn't this sad, Annabelle?" I said. As the movie went on I exclaimed two, perhaps three times more how sad the situation of the fox was, until she, Annabelle, turned to me and said, "Don't worry so much, Grandpa, it's only a movie." Another time, noting her watching a rather dullish kids' show called *Barney & Friends*, I asked what she found interesting in the show. "I know its stupid, Grandpa, but I get ideas from it," she said. Not yet four years old, she was already the artist in training.

Annabelle was occasionally taken to a Black evangelical church with her Aunt Millicent and Uncle Jack. When I asked her what went on there, she said, "Everyone keeps saying, 'Hallellulu.'" I taught her a few words of Yiddish: among them *kepi* for "head," *punim* for "face," *tuches* for "rear end." "*Tuches,*" I said, "as in *tuches* a long time to get there." Four years old and she got the joke. She got all the jokes. I once took her to lunch at the Northwestern University student union cafeteria. At the checkout line, I asked, "Would you like some potato chips to go with your lunch, sweetie?" Settled at our table, she said, with a look of great earnestness, "Grandpa, please don't call me 'sweetie' in public."

Annabelle spent all her weekends with us. She later told me that she couldn't wait for the weekends to arrive. She and Barbara spent lots of time together, much of it at our kitchen counter drawing, filling in coloring books, making what they called "concoctions" with different foods. Annabelle became the daughter Barbara never had, and Barbara became Annabelle's second mother. It was lovely to see.

Once, when I was at her mother's apartment in Hyde Park, the five-year-old Annabelle called out from the living room window overlooking Cornell Avenue, "There's Ingrid [a girl her own age who lived next door]. Ingrid has a daddy." Hearing her say this, I was determined to do what I could, within the confines of my own life, to give her, Annabelle, a replacement for her own lost father.

We took Annabelle to Disneyland. Another time we took her to San Francisco, where we stayed at the Ritz and bought her a white terry-cloth robe with "Ritz" sewn in over the left breast pocket. We spent a weekend together at Galena, Illinois, a Midwest vacation spot. When she was thirteen, I taught her to drive, three years before she could get a license, in a nearby Catholic cemetery, where I had years before attended the funeral of James T. Farrell. Barbara regularly took her shopping for clothes.

I sent Annabelle to private schools. She went to a Montessori school in Hyde Park. For high school she went to St. Scholastica Academy, where, alas, Catholic education is no longer what it once was: she wasn't required to take Latin, she had no nuns for teachers, the theology course did not pose such questions as why is there suffering in the world, how to prove the existence of God, or what is evil, but instead had students feed the homeless and keep a journal about it. Once, she received a card in the mail from one of her teachers that read "Thank you for trusting me." When I asked her what that was about, she replied, "Oh, Ms. Brash sent that card to everyone. She's a jerk." She did have an art teacher there who recognized and encouraged her obvious artistic talent. Annabelle lived with us through her high school years. After high school she went to the American Academy of Art. Later she found her métier in the design and fabrication of jewelry and has ever since run a successful business doing that.

When she was a young woman, Annabelle once told me that she could say things to me that she couldn't say to anyone else. I felt greatly complimented by this. I also felt I could speak to her with absolute candor. An old Freudian joke has it that the reasons grandparents and grandchildren get along so well is that they have a common enemy. Annabelle and I have always gotten along splendidly, no enemy needed.

Two summers ago, I fell—spoiler alert, old guys tend to fall—and fractured my right leg's femur, that long bone that runs from above the knee to the pelvis. I had to have surgery and spent three days afterward in an orthopedic hospital. When I left the hospital I was bound to a wheelchair. I needed help to do nearly everything I once did without thought. Annabelle, who was living in Jersey City, arrived, leaving her husband, Martin, alone, and stayed for a full month, shopping, cooking, helping Barbara take care of me in countless ways. For that month my granddaughter became, in effect, my mother. Without her help I might have been forced to go into rehab. The following month, my son Mark arrived for one of his visits to his second home, now in nearby Skokie, and he, too, did all sorts of things on my behalf. During this time, a granddaughter and a son coming to my much needed aid, I felt the full benevolent force of family, and a fine feeling it was. The term "support system" came alive, and in my granddaughter and son it seems I had one of the best.

Chapter Thirteen

Freelance

A week or so before I left Britannica I flew to Boston for an interview for a job at the *Atlantic* magazine. The interview was conducted over lunch at the Ritz-Carlton by the editor of the magazine, a man named Robert Manning, who ordered a carafe of wine with our lunch. I set out to explain what I thought I could do for the magazine, which was to raise the quality of its coverage of books and the arts, offering a plentitude of names and examples both of subjects and writers. Before I had gone halfway through my spiel, Manning had ordered a second carafe of wine, and it became clear that he hadn't been listening to anything I had been saying. I might have finished what I had to say in a strong Yiddish accent, which I was tempted to do, for so far gone was he, he wouldn't have noticed. A week or so later I received a rather formal letter from him saying he was sorry but he didn't think me quite right for the job.

I finally did arrange a job, working with Ivan Dee at a Chicago publishing firm called Quadrangle Books. I say "working with" when I was really working for Ivan, but he was so gracious that he never for a moment made me feel an employee. My job was to solicit manuscripts, which I would then edit. I was able to sign on books from, among others, the film critic Vernon Young, the political scientist Hans Morgenthau, the social scientist Robert Nisbet, the novelist Albert Halper, and the civil rights leader Bayard Rustin. I shall always remember Vernon Young for replying to someone who, upon first meeting, called him by his first name, to which he replied, "My good friends always call me Mr. Young. Won't you do likewise?" I recall Hans Morgenthau's small but elegant Lexington Avenue apartment, with its rich oriental rugs, a touch, I thought, of the Weimar Republic. Robert Nisbet, generally so cheerful and with a winning smile, found himself so dismayed at the turn the world had taken that he went into a hermit-like isolation in the last year or so of his life.

The Rustin manuscript, a collection of essays, came by way of my friend Midge Decter, who knew Rustin well. I met Bayard Rustin only once, at his office at the A. Philip Randolph Institute in New York. He was most impressive and is said to have been the main organizing hand for the famous 1963 civil rights march on Washington. Because as a young man Bayard had been a member of the Young Communist League and had been picked up more than once for lewd (i.e., homosexual) behavior, he maintained a behind-the-scenes position in the civil rights movement, an eminence quite gray but not less eminent for that. "I know now that for me sex must be sublimated if I am to live with myself and in this world any longer," he had earlier written.

My one meeting with Bayard came when he was organizing another march on Washington. Telling me about it, he brought up

Ralph Abernathy, who was thought to be a close friend of Martin Luther King Jr. in the civil rights movement.

"You know, Joe," Bayard said, "when Martin won the Nobel Prize, Ralph thought he had won it, too. He would show up for dinners in Stockholm to which he wasn't invited, get in limousines that weren't ordered for him. I suppose Martin must have thought himself lucky he didn't bring his mules to Stockholm." Abernathy in those years used to bring his farm mules to protest marches.

Rustin went on to tell me of a recent conference call with Martin Luther King Jr. in Atlanta, Whitney Young in Chicago, Roy Wilkins and himself in New York, and Ralph Abernathy in Virginia. "We were discussing this forthcoming march on Washington when we heard a snoring sound on the phone. 'Martin,' I said. 'Here,' Martin answered. 'Whitney?' 'Here.' And so on, except for Ralph, who was snoring happily away and continued to do so through our hour-or-so-long call. You know, Joe, in any protest movement there are some people who are only good for going to jail. Ralph is one of them. I only hope he doesn't bring those fucking mules to Washington."

Life at Quadrangle Books was agreeable enough, chiefly owing to Ivan Dee, who was not only excellent at his work but who had a splendid sense of humor. The firm was located in a small house on Delaware Place on Chicago's Near North Side. At the corner was a restaurant called Carton's, a greasy spoon of the kind with which Chicago was once heavily populated and which Ivan always pronounced "Car-tone" with a strong fake French accent. When going off to lunch, he would tell one of the office secretaries, "I shall be at my regular table at *Car-tone*." One day I joked with him about the danger of his growing punchy from too lengthy sessions of copyediting, and the next day he came out of his office, shadowboxing, snuffling, wearing a new pair of Everlast boxing shoes. At one point I bought a catcher's mitt and Ivan brought a baseball mitt from home, and we would have a twenty-or-so-minute catch in the parking lot behind the office after lunch. I not only found a pleasing job at Quadrangle but a lifelong friend in Ivan.

Another advantage that came of working at Quadrangle is that while there I came to know the literary agent Georges Borchardt. Georges was German by ancestry, French by nationality, and international by manner. I first encountered him on behalf of a Quadrangle author whose agent Georges was. I was much impressed by the orderliness of his mind, by his somewhat dry wit, by his power of subtle negotiation. He was, somehow, able to make one feel one's own financial offer for a manuscript was rather paltry without quite being insulting while doing so. Not long after this first meeting, I asked Georges if he would agree to become my agent. He did, and we have worked together, without disagreement, for more than fifty years.

I might have remained a good while at Quadrangle, but the firm was soon bought out by the New York Times Company. The man put in charge of overseeing Quadrangle for the Times was Herb Nagourney. Small, often displaying wet underarms, no beauty by any measure, Nagourney was a skirt-chaser extraordinaire, a man with whom you would not feel safe leaving alone with your great-grandmother. He once told me the story of coming home one evening to find his latest lady friend, a secretary at the *Times*, in his living room explaining to his wife that he, Herb, intended to leave her, his wife, and go off with her, the lady friend. When I asked him what he did about this domestic catastrophe, Herb said, "What could I do? I got rid of the secretary as quickly as I could, and promised Ruthie [his wife, whose name he pronounced Rooty] that I would go back into therapy."

As for Herb Nagourney's knowledge of the book business, one day in a meeting to discuss the new publishing season, he announced that the New York Times Company had just bought the magazine *Golf Digest.* "I note that Quadrangle has a number of books about boating on its backlist," he said. Here he paused, touched the knee of a man named Dick Crane, the firm's recently hired business manager, and said, "Excuse me, Dick, for what I'm about to say, but I recommend we put adds for our sailing books in *Golf Digest.* I know these goyim: if they golf, they sail."

Before long the New York Times Company decided to move Quadrangle to New York, where it would become Quadrangle–New York Times Books, Inc. I was invited along. "Things don't work out," it was reported to me that Herb Nagourney said, "we can always use Joe on the paper's cultural pages." In those days, Hilton Kramer was an art critic on the *New York Times*, and he regularly filled me in on the hijinks and generally nuttiness of life at the paper; it was like having a personal spy in the Kremlin. I recall once visiting Hilton there and passing by the cubicles of once well-known journalists no longer given anything deemed important to write about, the journalistic equivalent of all dressed up but with nowhere to go. No, I quickly decided that I did best to steer clear of working for the *New York Times.*

Around this time, in the spring of 1970, I wrote an essay that was published in the September 1970 issue of *Harper's* under the rather awkward title of "Homo/Hetero: The Struggle for Sexual Identity." My own title for the essay, "The Queer Thing," was much more casual. After the essay's publication, *Harper's* received some four hundred letters about it, mostly of complaint. (In an age of online, the number would surely have been well above forty thousand clicks.) A sit-in was staged about the essay at *Harper's* office. A man named Merle Miller wrote a book, *On Being Different: What It Means to Be a Homosexual*, in reaction to it. Today, more than fifty years after its publication, people who disagree with other of my views often drag this essay in to use against me. A paragraph in my Wikipedia entry is given over to it.

What motivated me to write the essay was nothing more than that I thought male homosexuality a rich subject, which it surely is, and one about which not much was really known. Not that I had any special knowledge of the subject myself. In the essay, I mentioned, as I have earlier in this book, a man who waited several hours outside a shop I worked at in downtown Chicago when I was sixteen to arrange an assignation with me. On another occasion, in Little Rock, the then mayor of North Little Rock, with whom I had been lunching and who had had four martinis with his lunch, attempted to kiss me in the men's room in the club at which we were lunching and from whose embrace I was easily enough able to extract myself.

The gravamen of my essay on homosexuality is that what causes it remains a mystery; it can bring much psychological sadness; in its social acceptance it is—or at least in that day was—accompanied by much hypocrisy. (Of the degrading remarks about the Kennedy White House cast by Truman Capote and Gore Vidal, the liberal Princess Lee Radziwill remarked to her sister Jacqueline Kennedy that she was not to worry, for Capote and Vidal were, after all, "just two fags.") Toward the close of my essay I wrote, "If I had the power to do so, I would wish homosexuality off the face of the earth," which was taken to mean, by Gore Vidal among others, in an argument ad Hitlerum, that I wished all homosexuals dead. Not at all. What I wished for homosexuals has, in fact, over the past fifty years become true—namely, their acceptance in the wider society, an acceptance so great that gay men and lesbian women now serve in high public office without the need to disguise their sexual proclivities. The widened tolerance and acceptance of homosexuality has been one of the few genuine hallmarks of social progress over the past half century.

In 1970 I was able to write this essay and have it published in a major American magazine. Despite the clamor it caused at the time of its publication, this did not stand in the way of my being offered a job teaching at Northwestern University a year or so later and not long after that the editorship of the *American Scholar*, the intellectual quarterly of Phi Beta Kappa. In our day none of these things—my writing the essay, *Harper's* publishing it, my being offered two rather cushy jobs after it appeared in print—would be possible. This, distinctly, does not mark progress, of any kind. Quite the reverse.

Apart from fifty-odd years of being accused of homophobia, my *Harper's* essay brought me sufficient confidence to think I could stay afloat as a freelance writer. I had, over the years, been publishing essays, stories, and reviews in the *New Yorker*, *Encounter*, *Commentary*, the *New Republic*, and other magazines. Time, I decided, to write a book. The book I wrote was *Divorced in America*, which carried the subtitle *Marriage in an Age of Possibility.* I received a $20,000 advance for writing it, half paid upon signing the contract, the other half when the book was completed. I was now, not in effect but in fact, a freelancer. And a freelancer of sorts I have remained. After 1970

I have never again worked in an office, which some might feel, as I tend to do, one definition of the good life.

Now that I was to work at home, I let go the nice woman who had been coming in to greet my four sons on their return from school and who prepared our dinners. I set up my clunky Remington standard typewriter on our apartment's enclosed back porch and went to work on the divorce book. As for the book's subject, I chose to write on it not only because I had myself recently gone through a divorce but because I felt that much nonsense had been written about it. A stellar example was a recent book with the title *Creative Divorce: A New Opportunity for Personal Growth*, by Mel Krantzler, a book that remained on the *New York Times* bestseller list for a full year and is said to have sold some three million copies. My own view was that divorce was creative all right, but what it chiefly created was havoc, sadness, and heartbreak for children.

What was becoming clear is that I seem to have a clear penchant for going against the grain of our times. As I wrote about the sadness of divorce, so I would later write books about the necessity of ambition ("the fuel of achievement," I called it), the complications of friendship, the pleasures of gossip, the positive aspects of envy. I prefer to think that this contrarian strain in my writing was not perverse, but instead a response to the goofy times more and more prevalent in the world in which I found myself.

I wrote my divorce book, as I seem to have written all my books, without an outline, but instead composing one paragraph after another, on the assumption that if all my paragraphs are interesting, so will my book be. As with other of my books, somewhere toward the middle of my divorce book I felt lost at sea—the same is true of this one—but too far out to turn, or to give the advance, back.

Divorced in America was chosen as a Book of the Month Club alternate, was published in England by the firm of Jonathan Cape, earned out its advance, and received pleasing reviews generally, though, as usual as part of that cranky fraternity known as authors, I seem to recall only a brief, somewhat negative one. This was written in the *New York Review of Books* by Margot Hentoff, wife of the jazz critic Nat Hentoff, and the offending (to me) passage read: "In *Divorced in America*, [Epstein] writes of what it means to be divorced and, in his case, in custody of his children. Mr. Epstein is a traditionalist, somewhat stuffy, often self-righteous—yet clearly a decent man. His wife left him because she was not happy—with him, with life at home with their sons. *Reading him, I can understand her reasons for wanting to leave* [my italics]. But I do not know how she could bear to go." *Argh*, so to speak, and *Oy!* I am reminded here of E. M. Cioran, that dark aphorist, who wrote: "As memory weakens, the praise that has been lavished upon us fades, too, to the advantage of the censure. And this is just: the praise has rarely been deserved, whereas the censure sheds a certain light on what we did not know about ourselves."

I continued to freelance with various magazines. Among them was *Dissent*, then edited by Irving Howe, another older man who took up my cause. Irving was then a leading literary critic, one with a strong political bent. (His best-known book was then *Politics and the Novel.*) He came out strongly against the New Left, but would never desert his own youthfully acquired desire for socialism. I wrote four essays for him: one on the working-class town of Cicero, Illinois; one on the newly arisen neoconservative movement; one on William F. Buckley Jr.; and an introduction to a collection of the best *Dissent* essays of the past twenty years. Irving cultivated young writers, and

I was still young enough—my early thirties—to be thought worthy of his cultivation.

I first met Irving when he arrived in Evanston to give a lecture at Northwestern University. He showed up at my apartment, a tallish man who had not gone to undue lengths about his grooming. I once described him to a friend as looking as if his shirt were out of his pants, even though it wasn't. I found intimacy with him easy. I once visited him at his office at the City University of New York, where a vast manuscript sat upon his desk. The manuscript was for what was to be his bestselling book, *World of Our Fathers.* "I'm told the book is likely to sell well," he said, quite without enthusiasm. When I asked him why this wasn't a pleasing prospect, he replied: "I've never got over a remark of Elizabeth Hardwick's that got back to me. 'Irving Howe,' she said, 'another Jew boy in a hurry.' The remark has haunted me."

On his Evanston visit, Irving suggested that I could nicely remove the pressures of the freelance life by acquiring an academic job. I told him I shouldn't mind that at all, but didn't see how I could bring it off since I had no advanced degrees. Neither, I knew, did he, though he was currently teaching at Brandeis. "Let me see what I can do," he said.

What Irving Howe did was somehow arrange to have the then head of the Northwestern English department, a man named Samuel Hynes, whose academic specialities were Thomas Hardy, the Auden generation, and World War II, in which he fought as a marine and later wrote about, call me in for a job interview. How Irving brought this off I never discovered. ("There's a young guy named Joseph Epstein, lives right here in Evanston, may just turn out to be important some day. You might think about offering him a job"?) At the interview, which went smoothly enough, Sam Hynes said that before he could make me a final offer I would need to give a talk to the English department faculty, which I agreed to do. The talk I gave was on the man of letters, which was what I fancied myself becoming, and, though less than dazzling, it seemed to come off well enough. The day after giving it I was offered a job teaching six courses—two courses in each of the school's three regular quarters—for an annual salary of $20,000.

Chapter Fourteen

A Job in the Neighborhood

In 1972 I called my mother to tell her that I had just been offered a job teaching at Northwestern University. "That's nice," she said. "A job in the neighborhood." And that is roughly what the job turned out to be. As it happened, I was then living six or so blocks from the university; I later moved to within two blocks of the school. But the larger truth is that, though I taught for thirty years at Northwestern, my years there never came to much more than a job in the neighborhood.

A strange place, Northwestern. When people used to ask me what is best about it, I answered, "Buildings and grounds and the quarterback coach." The school is just on the wrong side of the cutting edge of snobbery. In that of *U.S. News & World Report* and other imprecise rankings, Northwestern usually ends up somewhere between the ninth and fifteenth best school in the country. Among many of its students, who dreamt of getting into Harvard, Yale, Princeton,

Stanford, I discovered the school was a second choice, a fallback position. After teaching there a short while, I realized that, with the correct stationery—letterhead of Harvard, Yale, Princeton—I could clear out the faculty in a week: "Dear Professor X, We are prepared to offer you a job at Harvard [Yale, Princeton], at $10,000 less than your current salary, but we must ask that you arrive on campus next Tuesday. . . ." Most of the faculty at Northwestern would have shown up on Monday night.

Nor did Northwestern, viewed strictly as an institution, have much in the way of character. In the bad old days, it had entrance quotas on Jews, Catholics and, of course, Blacks. (When, as an undergraduate, I applied to the University of Chicago, I also applied to Northwestern, and was accepted at the former, while rejected at the latter.) When the social winds changed, it did, too, and was—and is—all for Diversity, Inclusivity, Equity, letters that, put together another way, spell D-I-E, and they may indeed go a long way toward killing the contemporary American university. Political correctness rules throughout Northwestern. In its humanities and social sciences divisions, gender, queer, and postcolonial studies are foremost. The school's fees, owing in part to its top-heavy DIE administrators, are among the highest in the country.

Some while before I arrived, Northwestern had given up its faculty club on Sheridan Road. This greatly limited my knowledge of faculty outside the English department, though I already knew Erich Heller, the critic of continental literature who taught in the German department, and Walter B. Scott, the parodist, who taught in the School of Speech, and both of whom I counted as friends. Ernest Samuels, the biographer of Henry Adams and Bernard Berenson, had retired the year before I began teaching at Northwestern, though I came to know him in a superficial way. Richard Ellmann, whom I knew and much liked, the biographer of James Joyce, W. B. Yeats, and Oscar Wilde, had been the star figure in the Northwestern English department, but he received one of those letters from Yale and departed in 1968, and later received an even better letter from Oxford, where he died in 1987.

By the time I began teaching, informality was the reigning academic tone. Younger teachers had begun teaching in jeans, more and more resembling their students, whom they addressed by their first names and in some cases were also so addressed by their students. Students now wrote formal evaluations of their teachers. Many teachers, at least the younger ones, were having sex with their undergraduate students. The professor as the figure of grand authority was out; the teacher as intimate guy, the pal, was in.

Before I began teaching I had two decisions to make. The first was what to wear to class; the second whether to address my students by their first or last names. I had no jeans, but lots of neckties and blazers and jackets, and decided to go with those. I thought dressing as an adult might give me a touch of authority, and also suggest that, if need be, I might be able to land a job elsewhere, at, say, a shoe store in the Loop.

As for how to address students, I hadn't quite made up my mind until I walked into my first class, an introduction to the novel, and began calling the roll, last names first. When I got to the name Pipal, Faustin, an earnest redheaded kid said, "Sir, do you mind calling me Frosty?" Instanter my decision was made. "I'm sorry, Mr. Pipal," I said, "but I address all my students by their last names."

No training exists for college teaching. One might have had a great, or at any rate highly effective, teacher during one's own days of formal education and try to imitate him or her. But I hadn't any such teacher on which to model my own teaching. Instead, I attempted to go into class and talk as interestingly as I could about the books or subjects I assigned. Along with courses on authors, chiefly novelists, I also taught a regular course on prose style and an occasional one on writing short stories. I hoped that my own strong distaste for boredom would help prevent me from boring my students. Whether or not it did is of course not for me to say.

Northwestern students had what I came to think the habits of achievement—that is, they did what was asked of them. Told to read a five-hundred-page novel over a period of five or six days, they did so. Asked to write a ten-page paper over a weekend, they produced the paper. They were what I came to think of as "good at school," a skill without any necessary carryover, like being good at pole-vaulting or playing the harmonica.

One of the significant differences between college teaching and that in high school or grammar school, is that in college one can teach to the best students in one's class, whereas for the earlier years a teacher is responsible for seeing that no student, however sadly inept, falls behind. Grammar school and high school teaching, I came to believe, are the Lord's work. College teaching comes closer to being a racket. "Welcome to the racket," Walter Scott said to me when I first began teaching.

What Walter meant was that college teaching was a relatively easy job. At Northwestern, one taught twenty-four out of the year's fifty-two weeks. I chose to teach ninety-minute classes on Tuesdays and Thursdays, thus leaving me free to attend to my own writing. (I always thought myself primarily a writer, only secondarily a teacher.) In other words, I was actually employed at the job 96 of the year's 365 days, adding in time for preparing for classes and grading student papers. As Walter said, a racket.

In my case it was made all the easier by my not being on a tenure track. I didn't have to produce scholarship to be sent off to refereed journals or turn out university press books that would establish my scholarly seriousness. Nor did I have to sit through tedious department meetings or serve on committees. I merely taught my classes and went home. As my mother said, a job in the neighborhood.

Not that I ever entered a classroom as a teacher completely free from nervousness. I worried about filling my full ninety-minute classes; I worried about boring my students (W. H. Auden defined a professor as "a man who talks in other people's sleep"); I worried about betraying inexcusable ignorance of one or another kind. I mentioned these worries to Saul Bellow, who himself came to teaching fairly late and who instructed me in my own teaching to think of myself as "casting artificial pearls before real swine."

I also wanted to get my message through, which was the seriousness and joyfulness of literature. I loved the authors I taught—James, Conrad, Cather, and a few others—and I wanted the best of my students to love them, too; and in loving them to understand how such writers could enlarge their view of life and ultimately enrich their own lives. I also put in a lot of time correcting my students' papers, from their misspellings to their faulty formulations, from their grammar to their larger misconceptions. Not that they are any accurate measure, but student evaluations of my teaching were generally approving, and often more than that. "Perhaps the best course I've taken in college."

"Top notch—the champagne of academic experience." "Each class period was among the shortest 90 minutes of my week. Interesting. Stimulating. Controversial." But the best student evaluation I received over thirty years of teaching read: "I did extremely well in this course, but then I would have been ashamed not to have done."

I never taught a class with more than forty or so students, and more usually seminars with only fifteen or so. Which meant I did not lecture my students, at least not for the full duration of my classes. Instead I opened my classes with twenty or so minutes of background information on the subject of the day, and spent the majority of the time questioning them, in the manner of a poor man's (though better dressed) Socrates. Some days these questions were more stimulating than others. ("We hav' vays of makin' you talk," I would say in my best Teutonic accent when a question failed to receive an interested response.) I meanwhile carefully prepared, perhaps overprepared, for all my classes, lest I seem shoddy or embarrass myself by not knowing a Latin tag or misunderstanding a crucial passage in one of the books I was teaching. I came to believe that the best education was to be had not as a student but as a teacher.

As for my teaching style, I like to think it was formal, earnest, with touches of irony, and occasional jokiness. I attempted to establish in my classrooms a sense of goodwill. Unlike the tough-guy tradition in teaching, I did not try to evoke fear in my students, while at the same time I tried to convey that I was not a man to fool with when it came to classroom conduct, deadlines for papers, and the rest.

The most popular teacher at Northwestern during my early years there was Bergen Evans, who was the host of a television show called *The Last Word.* Four and five hundred or so students attended his survey courses in world literature. If you were an engineering or chemistry or physics student, Bergen Evans's was probably the one literature course you took. I attended one of his lectures—on the *Iliad*, which he delivered seated on a chair on an ample stage—and found it rather commonplace. Not long after, a student in one of my writing courses told me that he was taking Evans's class in American usage, and three times during the course Evans reached into his jacket pocket to take out and read from a letter he claimed to have received the day before—only all three times it was the same letter. Bergen Evans died in 1978, at the age of seventy-three.

Over the years I had perhaps fifty or so extraordinary students. These were young men and women who sensed that something more was at stake in their education than a good grade. Among them were Donna Rifkind, who has written much intelligent criticism and an elegant biography of Salka Viertel and the exiles from Nazi Germany living in California; the poet and translator Joshua Weiner; the *Wall Street Journal* book review editor David Propson; the political journalist and longtime editor of the *Washington Monthly*, Paul Glastris; the journalist Julie Zimmerman, who as an undergraduate wrote so brilliant an essay about alcoholism in F. Scott Fitzgerald that I published it in the *American Scholar*; the novelist Karen Russell; the senior rabbi of the Wilshire Boulevard Temple in Los Angeles, Steven Leder; Jonathan Eig, the biographer of Lou Gehrig, Jackie Robinson, Muhammad Ali, and Martin Luther King Jr.; the founding president of the University of Austin, Pano Kanelos; and Robert Messenger, who worked as an editor, specializing in the arts and culture, at the *New York Sun*, the *New Criterion*, the *Atlantic*, the *Weekly Standard*, and the publishing firm of Simon &

Schuster, where, in a nice reversal of teacher and student, he has edited the book you are now reading.

Doubtless owing to the changed atmosphere in universities since the student riots of the last half of the 1960s, standards, at least in the humanities and social sciences, had loosened and slipped downward. This was reflected, as I have mentioned, in classroom behavior, in professorial dress, and in calling students by their first names. (I sometimes wished on the first day of class, after writing my name and office hours on the board, to turn to tell students to feel free to call me Frosty.) More important, it was shown in the new generosity in grading. Lots of A's were now given out. To give a student a B was rather a gentle put-down, a C a direct insult. I once had a female student cry in my office about what she thought the harshness with which I graded her final paper. "Charlie is never so hard on me as you are," she sobbed. ("Charlie?" *Might Charlie be bonking her?* I wondered.) Another time I had a call from a mother asking me to explain why I had given her daughter a B in my course on Willa Cather. "Tiffany always gets A's," she explained. I couldn't convince her that, in my courses at least, a B was an honorable grade.

God alone knew what went on in other classrooms. A graduate student once came to me to ask if I thought Dickens's character David Copperfield was a sexual criminal. When I asked why she might think that, she answered that Professor X said in class that Copperfield was a sexual criminal because he had made his first wife, Dora Spenlow, pregnant, from which, after miscarrying, she eventually died. I wanted to say, *What nonsense!*, but remembered one shouldn't knock a colleague. So instead I merely said, "Ah, Marnie, we sleep tonight. Criticism stands guard." In a class of my own, I asked a student to describe Gilbert Osmond from Henry James's *The Portrait of a Lady*. Without intending to shock his classmates or me, he answered, "He's an asshole." I wish I had had the quickness of wit to have responded to him by saying, "I'm glad, Mr. Stern, that I didn't ask you to describe Oedipus."

I had another clue about what was going on in other classrooms when, upon passing out the reading list for the course I gave on Henry James, a student asked, "How would you like us to read these books?" When I asked what he meant, he replied: "You know, for their Marxism, feminism, deconstruction, whatever." I told him he and the rest of the class ought to read them to discover James's meaning, which would give them quite enough to do.

In my day as a student, I had no idea of any of my professor's politics, though I assumed that, in 1956, most were likely to have voted for Adlai Stevenson over Dwight Eisenhower. (One faculty member at the University of Chicago in those days, the historian Walter Johnson, was in fact cochairman of the 1952 National Committee for Stevenson for President.) But now, thanks to the sixties, professors felt free to openly bring their own politics to the classroom—and, more dramatically, to practice them out of the classroom.

An extreme case of this turned up at Northwestern during my time there when a teacher named Barbara Foley not only taught her politics—a standard version of Marxism—but also recruited students for a group called InCAR, standing for International Committee Against Racism. Herself born into the upper middle class, the daughter of a Columbia University professor, Foley had signed on for a lifetime struggle for revolution. She marched in every protest march, many of which she led; spoke through her bullhorn across the campus

("They're cutting off the breasts of women in Nicaragua"); set her student acolytes in InCAR to arguing their political views in other classes and proselytizing other students, all known to the university administration, none formally disapproved of by it.

Until an incident that took place on the evening of April 13, 1985, at Northwestern. InCAR students shouted down and threw blood, or at any rate some red liquid, on a speaker named Adolfo Calero, the commander in chief of the Nicaraguan Democratic Force, also known as the contras, then opposed to the strongly left-wing government in the country. Before the talk, Barbara Foley took the stage to announce that "Calero had the blood of thousands on his hands and no respect for the rights to life and free speech of people he helped to slaughter with the CIA's help." She claimed that as such "he had no right to speak," and "we are not going to let him speak," and he "should feel lucky to get out alive."

Foley was censured by a university committee for her actions on that night, found guilty of eight of eleven charges brought against her. The punishment following the censure was mild: a formal letter of reprimand and a warning that a repetition of such an action could result in her dismissal. As it happened, Barbara Foley, an assistant professor at the time, was up for tenure that year—tenure, which meant a permanent position on the faculty that could only be removed if one were guilty of one or another kind of moral turpitude. Tenure is generally granted on three grounds: teaching, scholarship, academic citizenship. The English department voted Barbara Foley tenure by a vote of ten to five. An outside committee also voted for her to get tenure. But at the end, her tenure was denied by the university's provost, an old-fashioned liberal named Raymond W. Mack, who claimed that, on the grounds of academic citizenship, he could not allow tenure to a faculty member who openly claimed not to believe in free speech.

An uproar followed, with much of the English department and most of Northwestern's faculty generally feeling that, though what Barbara Foley did to Adolfo Calero was wrong, what was done to her was worse. But Ray Mack's decision held. In the end, Foley departed Northwestern for Rutgers in Newark, in that day a Valhalla of sorts for academic radicals.

I wrote an essay about the Foley affair called "A Case of Academic Freedom." In it I attempted to show how misguided the notion of academic freedom had become. Originally academic freedom was the freedom for university teachers to hold whatever political opinions they wished outside the classroom, but it was never the freedom to impose these opinions on their students. The essay also took up the sad hypocrisy of much of the faculty and especially the English department at Northwestern over the Foley affair in attempting to defend the indefensible.

Such an essay, I realized, was scarcely likely to increase my popularity. As I walked the halls at Northwestern, my colleagues when passing me didn't know where to put their eyes. I had only one confrontation about my essay, and this was with an old friend, going back to high school days, who was then chairman (oops! I mean "chair," of course) of the English department and who had come out for Barbara Foley getting tenure. When I quizzed him about it, it became apparent that if he were to oppose Foley he would be in danger of losing the regard of his fellow teachers and graduate students. I suggested this was a less than courageous stand. "Are you calling me a coward?"

he asked. "I guess I am," I replied. This was thirty-nine years ago, and, sadly, we haven't spoken since.

I am a writer, and what was the point of writing if not to express one's own views without fear? In fact, I rather doubled down and not long after this published another essay, this one titled "The Academic Zoo: Theory—in Practice," about the subversion of the teaching of literature through those fashionable French importations that went under the name of deconstruction. Finally, still in the category of shooting myself in my own feet, when in Los Angeles on a panel of intellectual magazine editors, I noted that America is two nations, one that twice voted Ronald Reagan president of the United States, and the other the academic that continued to think Marxism a lively and viable mode of thought. I went on to mention that Northwestern was currently attempting to hire a Marxist teacher named Frederic Jameson, and in the attempt to get him, Northwestern had also offered his wife a job. I added, jokingly, that there is a rumor going about that Northwestern was also offering the Jamesons' dog $18,500 to guard the school's Patten Gymnasium. The remark got into the *Los Angeles Times* and other papers. That year my raise in pay at Northwestern was a piddling $400.

As a teacher without tenure, in effect a permanent visiting lecturer, I was each year presented with a letter from the office of the dean of the arts college proposing that I stay for yet another year and setting out the raise in my salary. Given all that I had written against the grain of the current-day English department and, indeed, academic life generally, why wasn't I not renewed, which is to say, fired? A number of members of the English faculty, I am told, proposed nothing less. Only in later years did I learn that the then president of the university, a man named Arnold Weber, a former labor economist from the University of Chicago, had sent out a diktat that Joseph Epstein was not to be dismissed. Arnold Weber died, at ninety, in 2020. I learned of his support too late to thank him.

The timing of my retirement from teaching, in 2002, when I was sixty-five, was, I must say, exquisite. Political correctness had not yet kicked in, at least not in the merciless way of today, nor were cell phones and tablets endemic. In the prose-writing course I taught, I used to give students a list of fifteen or so items—the Spanish Civil War, the 1913 Armory Show, Leon Trotsky, Paul Verlaine, Reynaldo Hahn, et alia—and ask how many items on the list they could identify. The number was invariably small. I told them that at their age I could not identify many of these items, either, but that if they wished to present themselves out into the world as cultured men and women they had to know about these items and a great deal more. Today the students could take that list and google all fifteen items in less than five minutes. But all they would have is information, not knowledge—let us not even begin to speak of wisdom. Digital culture, with its emphasis on pure information, and which looks to be here to stay, is in some ways anti-educational, and I am glad to have escaped contending with it as a teacher of the young.

The handwriting was on the wall, also the floor, the ceiling, and all the doors—political correctness and woke ideology generally make the contemporary university uninhabitable for anyone who wishes to think freely. I had had indications of this myself when I taught a course on the sociology of literature to would-be writers in the early 1990s. One of my first assignments was to ask students to study and report on a contemporary magazine. The young feminists in the class seemed to be interested only in the number of women who contributed to the magazines they were assigned. In a course I taught on Joseph Conrad, a graduate student told me that a friend of his girlfriend who was taking the course noted that in class I called on more male than female students. I told him to report back to her that I would call on a hermaphroditic armadillo if I thought it had anything interesting to say. I was glad to be gone from such a petty yet genuine tyranny.

Nearly twenty years after I had been formally retired from teaching at Northwestern, I was canceled, first by the Northwestern English department, then by the university at large. The reason for the cancellation was an op-ed I wrote in the *Wall Street Journal* humorously instructing Jill Biden, the wife of the new president, to cease calling herself "Dr. Biden." I suggested doing so on the grounds that calling oneself doctor when one wasn't a physician or a dentist was pretentious, and in her case, with an advanced degree in education, an EdD, also more than a touch silly. This op-ed, which I wrote not out of any strong feeling, but quite as much out of amusement, unleashed vast, quite unanticipated hatred upon me, this measured by the response I received from email, phone calls, Twitter comments, derogating online reviews of my most recent book, false attacks on my teaching, and more. The major charge against me, drawn from the always-full Woke buffet of charges (racism, homophobia, transphobia, etc.), was misogyny. I was, I now learned, a woman hater, showing, in fewer than eight hundred words, contempt and ingrained prejudice for women generally. Email on the matter let me know that I was better off dead, an "impotent old bastard," and (my favorite) a "Jewish cunt." Arnold Weber was long off the scene as president of Northwestern, and the then current president, a man named Morton (call

me "Morty") Schapiro, who in his official pronouncements spoke in pure platitudinese and made no intellectually challenging decisions, was not about to come to my aid.

In fact, this so-called cancellation never really laid a glove on me. I was of an age when I no longer looked for jobs, and my friends (many women among them) knew the charge of misogyny was preposterous. I even felt slightly honored by the cancellation. I wrote an essay on the subject, "The Making of a Misogynist," which I published in *Commentary.* In the writing life, nothing, not even virulent personal attacks, goes to waste.

I taught for thirty years at Northwestern and emerged from the experience without a friend, with the single exception of Gary Saul Morson (of the Department of Slavic Languages and Literatures). Thirty years and one friend. I do not think of myself an unfriendly fellow, but might I be wrong? Or might it be that the writing life, if one is to live up to its obligation to be forthright in all one writes, is not the most smoothest road along which to make lots of friends.

Chapter Fifteen

Let Them Grow Older

Yet another older friend, Hilton Kramer, nine years older than I, arranged for me to become editor of the *American Scholar.* I don't know how it came into my hands, but I discovered his two recommendations on my behalf to the journal's search committee for a new editor. These recommendations are so splendid that, had I been on the Phi Beta Kappa search committee and read them, I should have hired myself.

After our brief time together on the *New Leader,* Hilton and I remained in touch, chiefly through letters, but also by my visits to New York and his to Chicago. Our rapport had been immediate; on my part it had grown into the deepest affection. I looked up to Hilton as I would have done to an older brother: to his learning, his intellectual courage, his wit. I dedicated an early book of mine, *Partial Payments,* to him with the following words: "For Hilton Kramer, a youngest son, who for more than twenty-five years has been my ideal older brother."

Hilton hated a lie, was death on pretension, a near genius at discovering hidden motives. One might not know this from his writings—he published two books, both collections of essays, many of them polemical in spirit—but he was a very amusing man.

He left his job as the principal art critic at the *New York Times* to found the *New Criterion*, an intellectual monthly devoted to the arts. Hilton told me that an essay of mine, surveying the past quarter century in literature, was the first he had accepted for his new journal. I continued to write for the journal as long as he was alive, always more than pleased to have his approval for my writing. I often wonder what Hilton would have thought of life today, of the incursions of political correctness on our culture, of the bumptiousness of Donald Trump, of the loss of significance of contemporary visual art and poetry.

In his recommendation for me as editor of the *American Scholar*, Hilton might have been writing about himself: I was "in possession of a distinguished style in which . . . a distaste for pomposity lives on easy terms with high seriousness." I was "never, moreover, a sucker for any of the more nonsensical doctrines of the sixties, and on more than one occasion displayed a remarkable intellectual courage. . . . The point I wish to make is that Epstein is a man who takes his liberalism seriously, and has rigorously resisted what he regarded as temptations from both the Left and the Right. His integrity is beyond question."

Hilton's strong recommendation put me on the short list for the job. On the same list, I later learned, were the academic Stephen Donadio, the political commentator and Johnson administration press secretary Bill Moyers, the publisher Paul Neuthaler, the poet and editor Reed Whittemore, the book editor Elisabeth Sifton (daughter of Rheinhold Niebuhr), and the critic Roger Shattuck. (The backup list of candidates included Peter Brooks, Herbert Mitgang, O. B. Hardison, and Garry Wills.) I myself would have chosen Roger Shattuck for the job, but, fortunately, I wasn't asked.

An interview with the Phi Beta Kappa search committee was arranged. I really didn't think myself in serious contention for the job, but suggested to Barbara that we fly to New York, have an early dinner after the interview, and return that same night.

As for the search committee doing the interview, I recall among its members the literary critic Robert B. Heilman, the historians Peter Gay and John Hope Franklin, and the president of the University of Virginia, Edgar Shannon. Because I didn't think the job likely to be mine, I was rather casual in my answers to the committee members' questions. When Edgar Shannon asked me what I would do for the young if I were editor of the *American Scholar*, I replied, "I would let them grow older." I have since wondered if that answer didn't in fact land me the job.

As for the *American Scholar*, I was not a regular reader of the journal, though I would glimpse copies in Barbara's apartment, for she, unlike me, was a member of Phi Beta Kappa. After we married, I used to say that I was myself a Phi Beta Kappa by marriage. The journal seemed to me dullish. Lots of big names wrote for it, but their contributions to it tended to be less than first rate. The only notable piece of the time that appeared in its pages was a satirical one by Richard Rovere, the *New Yorker*'s Washington correspondent, mocking the then fashionable notion of an American Establishment. But much that the journal ran seemed like writing that ought to have been consigned to permanent life in the bottom drawers of desks, but was instead, what the hell, sent to and printed by the *American Scholar*.

Under the title of the journal, on its first page, in small print, was a quotation from Ralph Waldo Emerson that ran "In the right state, he is *Man Thinking*." I disliked Emerson, the pomposity of his prose style and those details of his personal life that I knew, and made a mental note to remove the quotation as quickly as possible, which, once editor, I soon enough did.

Hiram Haydn, my predecessor, had had the job for nearly thirty years, from 1944 to 1973, when he died of a heart attack. A busy man, Hiram began as a book editor, first at Crown, then at Bobbs-Merrill, then at Random House, where he became editor in chief in 1956. Three years later he departed to found, with Simon Michael Bessie and Alfred Knopf Jr., Atheneum Books. Five years after that, he left Atheneum to work for Harcourt, Brace & World. He earlier took a PhD from Columbia, went on to teach at three or four schools, and found the time and energy to write five rather hefty novels. All this while he was the editor of the *American Scholar.* My guess is that so much else was going on in his career that he hadn't much time for the journal, or at least that it was never his primary interest.

I'm not sure but that Phi Beta Kappa itself did not consider editing the quarterly *American Scholar* as more than a half-time job. My salary upon taking the editorship was $20,000, or half that of a full professor of the day. This sum allowed me to cut my own teaching down to three courses a year, or half time. The understanding was that I would not work in the Phi Beta Kappa offices off Dupont Circle in Washington, D.C., but remain in Evanston, visiting the Washington office three or four times a year. I would answer to the Phi Beta Kappa Senate, a group chiefly composed of two dozen academics, and to the organization's secretary and CEO, an amiable fellow named

Kenneth M. Greene. I would have two assistant editors to help me in dealing with contributors, copyediting, proofreading, and other of the nuts-and-bolts details needed to put out a journal. I was also allotted $4,000 for secretarial help in Evanston. All this was set out in a letter from John Hope Franklin, to which I responded by writing "that I accept your invitation—with gratitude, with enthusiasm, with a feeling of high intellectual excitement."

Now that I had a journal to edit, I realized that I did not have all that clear a notion of what ought to go into it. I had no program I wished to advance, as the editors of *Partisan Review* once wished to advance Marxism in politics and modernism in the arts, or the editors of the *Kenyon Review* wished to advance the New Criticism. I had no "line," no strong political views, no central idea that I felt crucial to the fate of the country or of the world. I merely had a great many things that, in an amateurish way (recalling that the root of the word *amateur* is "lover") interested me.

My first thought was that, as a quarterly, the *American Scholar* could not hope to keep up with the news or trends of the day, so why bother attempting to do so? That news was chiefly political and could be excluded from the journal's pages without loss. During my time as editor of the journal, no current occupant of the White House was mentioned in its pages. I was also chary of the various academic "isms" then flying around, from Marxism to Foucaultism. Straight literary criticism, of the kind that explained a work or ranked writers, I excluded as among the verboten. I also decided not to run any contemporary movie or art criticism. I ran a series of essays on great teachers written by their by now equally well-known students, which later came out as a book under the title *Masters*, a title doubtless unacceptable today when even "master bedroom" is outlawed. I ran odd pieces on working in bookstores or as a supernumerary in an opera company. I understood that many of my contributors would be academics, but I intended to get work from them that rose above the purely academic.

I hoped to make each issue as good as I could make it. In this regard, I had acquired an essay by Sidney Hook about his teacher at the City College of New York, Morris Raphael Cohen. When I told Sidney I planned to run the essay in our forthcoming summer issue, he replied that he wished I could hold it for the autumn issue, since no one reads summer issues of magazines. I told him that, with only four issues a year to run in a quarterly, I hoped he was mistaken, and besides, the essay was already scheduled. A month or so later Sidney wrote to tell me that he was wrong, for the response to his essay was ample and pleasing. I told him that I was delighted to hear it, not least because I could now claim to have bested Sidney Hook in an argument.

In many ways, an ideal contribution to the *American Scholar* in my time as its editor was an essay published in the summer 1978 issue under the title "On Reading Books: A Barbarian's Cogitations." The barbarian in question was the Harvard professor of economics, Alexander Gerschenkron; his subject was how to choose what books to read in a world of endless books and limited time. Professor Gerschenkron may have earned his living through teaching and writing about economics, but a most well-read and well-rounded fellow he turned out be. The range of reference in the essay, from Goethe to a detective novel called *The Body with a Missing Toe*, is most impressive.

In the essay Gerschenkron claims to have read *War and Peace* no fewer than fifteen times, "and at least twice I began rereading *War and Peace* at once, starting again after having read the last page." He offers three criteria for a good book: that it must be interesting, memorable, and rereadable, yet realizes that "one has to read a book before our criteria can be applied to it. An apple has to be bitten into before we know it is sour and should be thrown away." Wise, witty, with erudition lightly worn, and on a subject of general interest, the essay represented what I wanted for an *American Scholar* under my editorship.

This same issue of the *American Scholar* contains essays by William Haley ("Will There Always Be an England?"), Jervis Anderson ("Black Heavies," on heavyweight boxers), Peter Stern and Jean Yarbrough ("Hannah Arendt," as a teacher), Dan Jacobson ("Literature in the University"), and Max Delbrück ("Mind from Matter?"), among others. The issue also had book reviews by Sidney Hook, Leon Edel, Edward Luttwak, and Eric Partridge.

Under the rubric "Life and Letters," the same issue had an essay with the title, playing off Freud's book on the subject, "Jokes and Their Relation to the Conscious" by a writer calling himself Aristides. I was Aristides, and before I was finished, would write ninety-two of these roughly 6,500-word essays at the front of the *American Scholar.* I took up the name Aristides after the Athenian political figure, who was formally ostracized because, it was said, the citizens of Athens grew tired of always hearing him referred to as Aristides the Just.

Writing those essays was, as we should say today, a game changer for me. I had published short stories, many book reviews, some formal criticism, a few biographical essays, but with the steady publication of these Aristides essays, I became an essayist. I continued to write stories and reviews, but it was as an essayist that I soon became best known, which was all right with me. The splendid tradition of English essayists includes Joseph Addison, Charles Lamb, William Hazlitt, Max Beerbohm, Desmond MacCarthy, and George Orwell, and it would please me to think that my own essayistic scribblings might have a place in that tradition. Whether they do or not is not of course for me to say, but a number of other people have said so, among them Karl Shapiro and Heywood Hale Broun in print and Jacques Barzun and Joseph Mitchell in correspondence. Twenty-two years ago, Jacques Barzun, in a note I prize, wrote to me:

> Like Lamb and Hazlitt you transform yourself into a being who stands at the right distance—not at the pool, and yet not far from it. One wants to know about you under the aspect of history, that is, not through direct sight but through the imagination. And I have the good sense that your prose style bears the same relation to good talk that theirs did 200 years ago. They were accused of writing Cockney English because they had given up 18th century diction and captured the tone of contemporary speech without reproducing its vagaries. But you had a harder time, because modern talk is pedantically abstract and cluttered with voguish phrases.

"But enough about me," as the caption from a favorite cartoon of mine has it, "what do you think about my book?"

When I first began editing the *American Scholar,* I was given a survey of readers' opinions of the journal. Some readers wanted more science in the journal, others less; some wanted more literary criticism, others felt that the literary criticism the journal ran was a bore; and so on and on. Not that I ever would have followed such a survey in my own editing of the *American Scholar*, but it reinforced me in my plan to apply to my editing of the journal the same overriding criterion I applied to my own writing. That criterion was to disregard the reader and chiefly interest myself. The assumption here is that I was not an entirely boring person and that what interested me was also likely to interest many other people.

If my editing of the *American Scholar* had any larger theme, it was that of upholding the tradition of the liberal arts, which was then under attack in various ways in the contemporary university: politically, intellectually, and theoretically (by the advocates of that body of obscurantist learning known as "theory"). As Paul Oskar Kristeller, the scholar of Renaissance humanism, prophetically wrote: "We have witnessed what amounts to a cultural revolution, comparable to the one in China, if not worse, and whereas the Chinese have to some extent overcome their cultural revolution, I see many signs that ours is getting worse all the time, and no sign that it will be overcome in the foreseeable future."

I decided that the way to keep alive the tradition of the liberal arts was to publish those writers, in America and England, who best represented it. Among those in that tradition from whom I was able get contributions to the *American Scholar* during my years as the journal's editor were H. R. Trevor-Roper, Jacques Barzun, Arnaldo Momigliano, Edward Shils, Hugh Lloyd-Jones, Mary Lefkowitz, Peter Brown, G. W. Bowersock, Kristeller himself, and others. I did less well by way of scientists, though a number of distinguished scientists served on the journal's editorial board, among them Freeman

Dyson, John Hall Wheelock, Subrahmanyan Chandrasekhar, and Jeremy Bernstein.

The historian Gertrude Himmelfarb, who in her role as the anti–Lytton Strachey had done so much in her writings to return the Victorian intellectuals to their rightful place of esteem, was always a helpful influence on the board. Edward Shils was perhaps most helpful of all my board members, aiding me in giving the journal an international feeling by bringing to it such writers as Elie Kedourie, François Furet, and Leszek Kolakowski. Edward, Arnaldo Momigliano, and I used to fly from Chicago together to and from *Scholar* editorial board meetings. Walking through O'Hare with them—Edward with his walking stick and portly figure, looking like a secular Father Brown, the five-foot-tall Arnaldo with his crushed hat and seeming as if he were wearing more than one suit—I felt as if we were the intellectual version of the Marx Brothers, with me as the rather colorless Zeppo.

The editorial board met three times a year, twice in New York, one in Washington, D.C. The meetings lasted an hour or so, with dinner afterward. In these meetings the current and forthcoming issues were described and discussed. Suggestions for articles and writers for future issues were proposed. Some board members were more helpful than others. Some could be difficult. Diana Trilling once used up much the better part of a meeting complaining about an article in the journal about her husband, Lionel, whom she referred to as L.T. (not to be confused with Leo Tolstoy). Edward Shils, after unsuccessfully trying to mollify her, said to me after the meeting, "I wish instead I had said to her, 'Jew, leave the public bath.'" Edward was also Jewish, but then the best anti-Semitic remarks are often made by Jews.

Lillian Hellman was on the board. She could be impressively

intelligent, except when her sentences contained the initials FBI or CIA, which many of them did, for she suffered from left-wing paranoia. Paul Freund, the Harvard professor who, it was said, was supposed to have ascended to the Jewish seat on the Supreme Court, but didn't because he failed to curry the favor of John F. Kennedy, was always a font of good sense and subtle humor. I was with him when he mentioned to Lillian Hellman that he planned to attend the Strasbourg Conference that summer. "Is that still run by the CIA?" Lillian asked. "I don't believe so," Paul answered. "The food isn't all that good." I have a lingering memory of Lillian at one of our dinners, half-soused, fork in one hand, lit cigarette in the other, looking hopelessly sad.

One day in the *Washington Post* I noted a photograph of a man named Jacob Stein in blazer, striped shirt, and correspondent (or two-tone) shoes juggling pins. I was at the time a juggler myself, so I called him to arrange a meeting. He invited me for drinks at the Cosmos Club. We talked about juggling, show business, and much else. I found him, a prominent lawyer, in every way simpatico. I asked if he would like to join the editorial board of the *American Scholar.* Without hesitation he said yes. Over the years we became good friends. Jake was one of the two lawyers representing Monica Lewinsky, though I am less than sure that he wanted to be remembered for that. In his office, along with many literary books, sat a large bust of Groucho Marx. Jake's last request of me was that I send him my set of juggling pins, which I did. Not long after he died at ninety-four.

On a cold day in October 1991 at the airport in Minneapolis, where I had arrived to speak at a meeting of the National Association of Scholars, I awaited a cab. None were in sight. Two men were in line ahead of me. Finally a cab arrived, and I heard one of the men tell the driver they were going to the Marriott Hotel, which is where I was headed. I asked if I could share their cab. They agreed. On the way to the hotel, they talked about the recent Clarence Thomas Supreme Court confirmation hearings in a way that I recognized as shrinkinese; I recall the word "autoerotic." I paid my share for the cab, and at the hotel got in the reception line, one of my fellow cab sharers standing behind me.

"Do you have a room for Joseph Epstein?" I asked.

"Wait a minute," the man behind me said. "Are you *the* Joseph Epstein?"

I allowed I was *a* Joseph Epstein.

"No kidding," he said. "I love your writing. You're my alter ego. This is going to sound like a bobby-soxer, but do you mind if I go up to your room with you?"

He turned out to a man named Paul McHugh, the chief of psychiatry at Johns Hopkins, and a man of enormous intelligence and great ebullience to go along with it. Not long after this meeting he wrote a brilliant essay for the *American Scholar* called "Psychotherapy Awry," in which he recounted the ways that psychiatric practice had gone wrong, among them supporting transgender surgery, which he thought would come to be known as "the lobotomies of the late twentieth century." Paul and I stayed in touch, and I later asked him to join the journal's editorial board. At a dinner in his honor, I called Paul "a manic impressive" and remarked on my never knowing a man so intent on relieving suffering and generally doing good in the world. He has been a dear friend.

I didn't do all that much editing of manuscripts for the journal.

Through editing, I long ago discovered, one could make a second-rate composition publishable, but not splendid. For the most part, contributors to the *American* Scholar wrote well. I continued to solicit work for the journal, but after two or three years, writers I admired began sending me their writings without my asking. When H. L. Mencken, then editor of the *American Mercury*, was praised for discovering talent, he replied that all he had to do was open the mail, by which he meant that in the *American Mercury* he had established a place wherein good writers wished to appear. I liked to think that perhaps the same was now beginning to be true of the *American Scholar.*

I did, though, bring many a linguistic prohibition to my editing of the magazine. This entailed my rather long list of prescriptivist peeves. I decided never to allow the words "impact" (except for car crashes) or "intriguing" (except for spying) into the journal; "special," "caring," and "sharing" were also proscribed. "Arguably" and other weasel words were ruled out. The word "indeed" was no longer allowed to appear at the head of sentences, and the phrase "in terms of" anywhere in any sentence. No "if you wills" or "as it weres" were permitted; the much overused "focus" was also barred, and no "whatevers" whatsoever. The words "process" and "values" were disdained, and "lifestyle" was put out to pasture. I called Max Delbrück, who won a Nobel Prize for his work in molecular biography, to ask him if he would mind removing the phrase "lifestyle of the cell" from his manuscript. "Ach," he said in his strong Teutonic accent, "I hate it, too, but zis is how ze idiots in ze field refer to it." I was slow to accept "Ms.," which I now find useful, and felt wary of the new use of "gay" to replace homosexual, on the grounds that this new usage would all but eliminate the fine old use of the word to mean lighthearted and carefree, which of course it has long since done.

Before long I began to be so identified with the *American Scholar* that it nearly became part of my name. People would introduce me by saying, "May I introduce Joseph Epstein, the editor of the *American Scholar.*" "You know Joe Epstein, don't you, he's the editor of the *American Scholar.*" Owing to my connection with the journal, I was made a trustee of the Hudson Institute and, a bit later, put on the council of the National Endowment for the Arts. All Hudson Institute trustees meetings began by the president of the institute, Herb London, going round the table and introducing each of the trustees. When he came to me, he said: "Joseph Epstein is of course the editor of the *American Scholar* and America's Montaigne." After he did this four or five times, I asked him to stop, saying, "Herb, forgive me, but whenever you refer to me as 'America's Montaigne,' I think of, but cannot imagine, Michel de Montaigne calling himself 'France's Joseph Epstein.' Please, I beg you, knock it off."

Mine was an ideal situation. I was editor of a quarterly journal that did not occupy my full time, leaving me the freedom to work on my own writing. (Along with other books, I was able to publish five collections of essays chiefly of my Aristides pieces.) In the Washington office of Phi Beta Kappa I had two excellent subeditors—Jean Stipicevic and Sandra Costich—who vetted over-the-transom manuscripts, dealt with galley and page proofs, worked with contributors, and much more. They did most of the work on the journal, while I got all the credit.

The *American Scholar* seemed to be flourishing. Lots of approving correspondence greeted each new issue. The circulation remained steady, at around twenty-five thousand readers. But, then, circulation is never a crucial measure of the success of an intellectual journal. As already noted, T. S. Eliot's *Criterion* never had more than six hundred readers. *Partisan Review*, perhaps the most influential of American little journals, lasted for sixty-nine years, but probably never had a circulation above five thousand. No, roughly twenty-five thousand readers, without any aggressive advertising campaign to raise that number, was, more than respectable, fairly impressive.

And then one day I received a phone call that suggested the possibility of increasing the readership, and possibly changing slightly the nature, of the *American Scholar* itself. The call was from a trustee of the Skirball Foundation, who reported that the foundation wished to make a substantial contribution to the *American Scholar.* The foundation's founder, Jack Skirball, a rabbi, movie producer, and real estate developer (an interesting trio of occupations), who had recently died, had been a devoted reader of the *American Scholar*, buying and sending out to friends some thirty subscriptions to the journal. The trustees thought it right that the foundation now help support the journal its founder had so admired. When I asked how much money it had in mind by way of support, my caller said, rather casually, "Somewhere in the low seven figures," which I took to be no less than $2 million.

I thought of all the things I could with the annual interest on the $2 million of Skirball money: raise contributors' fees, set young writers on special projects, perhaps find another few thousand readers for the journal. A few weeks later I went to New York to meet with the trustees of the Skirball Foundation to lock things down. They found my ideas agreeable. The deal, it seemed, was done.

And, then, the senate of Phi Beta Kappa voted to reject the journal receiving the $2 million of Skirball money. They felt the money was little more than a plot to secure my position as editor of the *American Scholar*, a notion that had never occurred to me. I knew I had enemies in the Phi Beta Kappa Senate, but naively had underestimated the intensity of their enmity. Part of this enmity derived from my refusal to run the standard feminist and African American victim pieces in the journal. I didn't do so because none that I received on either subject ever rose above the level of cliché. I ran essays by Black writers—Ralph Ellison, Martin Kilson, and Jervis Anderson among them—but none were about the wretchedness of America. I took no count of how many women writers I published, but then I never accepted a manuscript because it helped me fulfill a quota. Frederick Crews appeared in the journal persuasively attacking the new school of theory that would soon help bring down the prestige of English departments, which may also have given offense. But perhaps a larger part of their loathing derived from their belief that I was a conservative, which in their view really meant a right-winger, while I preferred to think myself, then as now, in that always small and powerless group known as the anti-bullshit party.

Not long after, I was fired from my job as editor of the *American Scholar*. I have recounted this firing in my last Aristides essay, which I titled "I'm History." In that essay, I argued that in small groups of liberals, radicals generally have their way. Orwell long ago made the point that liberals dread few things more than not being thought on the bus by people to the left of them. In the case of my being fired by the Phi Beta Kappa Senate, three people led the charge: one a historian of Black life, another a feminist specialist in gender studies, the third, a feminist who specialized in medieval history. They loathed me, I gathered, because I did not take their work seriously; no more serious insult, I suppose, than for an ostensibly serious person not to be taken seriously.

The vote against me was unanimous, but for one person, Eugen Weber, the historian of fin de siècle France, who, it was reported to me, in the meeting said, "I cannot vote against Joe. He is my friend." The official account, given to the *New York Times*, was that I had been fired because the journal was losing circulation and in search of younger readers. An editorial appeared in the *Wall Street Journal* in my defense and so did an article in the *Baltimore Sun*. But the valedictory words I most appreciated came from a man I did not know, a molecular biologist at MIT named Sheldon Penman, who, in a letter to the *Wall Street Journal*, wrote that "four times a year Mr. Epstein's gem arrived, a welcome relief from the intellectual drivel delivered in corrupt grammar that I have come to view as an occupational hazard. The *Scholar*'s unadorned, slightly pulpy pages, blessedly free of tarted up graphics, were redolent of another age when style and content really mattered. And style and content it most surely delivered. Few could have failed to have their minds stretched by its extraordinary reach delivered in impeccable and gracious writing." The letter ends by noting that I was fired because my contributors and I spoke our minds, which he suspected, rightly, was what "in the end sealed his fate."

Soon after I departed the *American Scholar*, Jake Stein told me that I would benefit from what he called "the Brooks Robinson factor." When I ask him what that was, Jake explained: "After Brooks Robinson retired from the Baltimore Orioles, the team acquired a new third baseman named Doug DeCinces, himself a darned good ballplayer.

But a foul ball would be hit, DeCinces would race seventy-five or so feet to his right, nearly fall down into the dugout, and barely miss the ball. One Oriole fan would then turn to the fan sitting beside him and say, 'Brooks would have got it.'" And so it proved. For years after my having been fired from the *American Scholar*, former readers would write to tell me that under my editorship so much of the stuff now being published in the magazine would never have been allowed. Brooks would have got it, in other words, and Joe would never have permitted it.

Chapter Sixteen

Hyde Parkers

Sometime in the early 1990s, I was invited to become a member of the Sojourners Club in Chicago by Michael Janeway. The club met the second Tuesday of every month to hear a twenty-or-so-minute talk. To become a member, one had to give one of these talks; I gave one on the subject of anecdotes. The Sojourners, I discovered, was an intellectual establishment of sorts, its members included the presidents and provosts of the local universities, the cardinal of the Chicago diocese and other clergymen, successful architects and physicians, academics who had cachet of some sort or other.

Michael Janeway was then the dean of the school of journalism at Northwestern. He was the son of Eliot Janeway (né Jacobstein), an economist who, in his day, was an adviser to Democratic politicians and had acquired fame as an economic forecaster on radio and television. Mike once told me that, at age fifteen, asked by his mother to clean out a closet in their Manhattan apartment, he discovered two things: that his father had been divorced and that he was Jewish. When he questioned his mother about why his father never mentioned his divorce, she told him: "You know Daddy doesn't like to talk about defeats."

Mike had an interesting résumé of his own. After graduating from Harvard, he worked for the *New Leader*, *Newsweek*, and the *Atlantic Monthly*. He next became an assistant to Cyrus Vance at the State Department during the Jimmy Carter years; and later was appointed editor of the *Boston Globe*, then the editor in chief of the publisher Little, Brown and Company, followed by Northwestern, and finally a professor at the Columbia Journalism School and a trustee of the Pew Foundation. I used to joke, to myself, that Mike was on the short list for prime minister of India and wrote a short story based on Mike Janeway that I called "Just the Man for the Job." He died, of cancer, a few weeks before his seventy-fourth birthday.

I went to Sojourner meetings for a year or so, and then dropped away. The talks tended to be boring and the company, with a few exceptions, not much better. One exception was a man named Henry Betts, a physician who was head of the Rehabilitation Institute of Chicago. Henry and I usually sat together during the Sojurner talks and dinners. One day he brought along two interns from the Rehabilitation Institute, introducing one to me as Billy Smith and the other by an Italian name I no longer remember. Toward the end of dinner, he gave Billy Smith a $10 bill and sent him down to the lobby to buy two Macanudo cigars. When he returned with the cigars, Henry paused a moment, then said, "Billy, my change." Billy turned out to be William Kennedy Smith, son of Jean Kennedy, the youngest daughter of Joseph Kennedy. He was later notorious thanks to a much publicized rape trial in which he was found not guilty.

One night at a Sojourner's Club meeting I was introduced to Edward Levi, attorney general under Gerald Ford and a former president of the University of Chicago. Levi, noted for the obliquity of his humor, said, "Ah, Joseph Epstein, the man everyone thinks teaches at the University of Chicago, but doesn't." Doubtless he meant that, because of my friendships with Saul Bellow and Edward Shils, some people might have thought I was, or ought to be, teaching with them in the Committee on Social Thought at the University of Chicago.

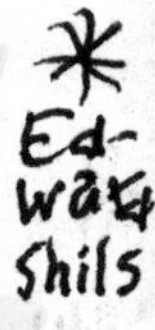

The mention of Saul Bellow and Edward Shils reminds me that, thus far along in this autobiography, I have not been strong on striking the confessional note. Perhaps this is owing to the fact that, not having anything all that interesting to confess, I never have been. In one of Saul Bellow's letters, to Leon Wieseltier, then the literary editor of the *New Republic*, he wrote: "Joe Epstein I like and respect but I don't open my heart to him because he doesn't have the impulse . . . to open up. Besides he's more fair-minded than we are, or more circumspect when he discusses our bogus contemporaries." Several years later Edward Shils told me how much he valued my friendship, even though, he said, "we do not talk of things of the heart." What I think Edward meant by this is that we never spoke to each other about our disappointments in life. I suspect that his were that he never wrote the single great book that would make his work of permanent interest to the world and that, twice divorced, he never enjoyed the pleasures of a full and happy family life. As for my own disappointments, they are too trivial to mention: that I cannot play the piano, that I wasn't a superior tennis player, that I never learned

ancient Greek, that when young I never owned a red convertible, or dated a ballerina.

One disappointment I do not have is never having undergone psychotherapy. I would not have been a good analysand, patient, customer. The therapeutic, based on the confessional, is not my mode. If a friend wishes to confess to me—and many have—I am honored by the trust and intimacy he is bestowing upon me with the act, but I do not feel it need be returned. We are all doubtless guilty of acts, either of commission or omission, we wish we hadn't committed or failed to commit. But the notion that life is a series of hidden defeats surely is mistaken. If it were true, we should all be in a state of more or less hidden depression, with life shorn of its amusement, the past dreadfully sad, the future immitigably dark.

I met Saul Bellow in 1972 when Harvey Shapiro, then editor of the *New York Times Book Review*, asked me to interview him. I was pleased to have this excuse to meet him, for I much admired his fiction. In those days Saul lived in a grand building in Hyde Park called the Cloisters and was between marriages numbers three and four (of five). I found him immensely intelligent, witty, not easily conned. He seemed to have taken the measure of his own talent and fame. He dressed expensively, in somewhat flashy clothes. Born in 1915, he was of the generation of men who did not go out without a hat. He was striking looking without being quite handsome, with an ample nose with flared nostrils that dominated his face, a deeply receded hairline, and a separation between his front teeth. "Never fall for a man with a separation in his front teeth," is the lesson his third wife took from their marriage.

Saul was twenty-two years older than I and his achievements vastly greater than mine, though from the outset I never felt any condescension in his treatment of me. We had in common an amused love for the city of Chicago, a passion for literature, a penchant for jokes, and an interest in the game of racquetball, which we soon played together.

I was pleased, delighted, proud even that Saul came to regard me as a friend. We lived twenty miles apart—he in Hyde Park, I in Evanston—but managed to get together once or twice a week, sometimes for meals, more regularly for racquetball, which we played at the Evanston YMCA, sometimes at the Riviera Club, of which he was a member. The Riviera Club had a number of members who were Syndicate, or Mob, guys, the most notable of whom was Gus Alex, said to be in charge of gambling and prostitution in the city. The athletic director was Max Ponder, whom I remembered as an All-State football player at Lane Technical High School.

Saul was nearly sixty when we played racquetball, and I sometimes worried he would have a heart attack during our games together. ("Nobel Prize Winner Dies in Racquetball Court," I imagined the headline reading, with the subhead "Man at Right in Shorts Unidentified.") His breathlessness did not deprive him of his wit. When I once reached a ball he thought a sure winner, he remarked, "Damn, you're quicker than a sperm."

We talked a fair amount about the New York intellectuals, Philip Rahv ("an old bull gone weak in the knees"), William Phillips ("the nice thing about *Hamlet* is that in it Polonius dies"), James Baldwin ("Jimmy, I fear, wants to be Martin Luther Queen"), Dwight Macdonald, Mary McCarthy, and others. He read to me from *Humboldt's Gift*, his novel then in progress, I offering the most minor of corrections. He told me that he recognized he wasn't the father he ought to be to his three sons—each with a different wife—but that writing his novels took up all the energy he had. I felt honored by his intimacy. The morning in 1976 that he won the Nobel Prize in Literature he called to tell me so. I looked forward to a long friendship with him.

One day Saul showed up at my apartment in Evanston with his friend Edward Shils. I had known of Shils, but only through his reputation as a teacher at the University of Chicago and through a few of his essays that I had read in *Encounter.* These essays, written in an unadorned prose and at a fairly high level of generality, might have been written by Max Weber and gave no hint of the extraordinary character of the man who wrote them.

For one thing, as Edward's prose was lean, his body was portly, though with nothing soft about it. While his writing was devoid of humor, his conversation was studded with it. That first day he checked the books in my bookcases, noted the prints and photographs on my walls and my houseplants. Why Saul thought we should meet I do not know, but I shall always be grateful to him for arranging our meeting. That night, we went to dinner at a Korean restaurant on Clark Street. Saul had brought along a lady friend, the writer Bette Howland, a contemporary of mine and soon to be a friend. Edward asked me what I was reading. When I said a novel by Alison Lurie, he replied, "Academic screwing, I take it." Quite right. Later in the meal, he asked me if it were true that Northwestern University had a strong African American studies program. When I said that I believed the school did have such program, he remarked: "Why, I wonder, would anyone wish to go to university to become a Negro."

In the current political correctness atmosphere, this will doubtless pass for a racist remark. I contend that it is the very reverse of racism. For one thing, "Negro" was the approved word of that day (1972). (Some might contend that things began to go wrong when Negroes insisted on being called, imprecisely, African Americans.) For another, more important thing, what Edward was really saying is what a shame that young Black students were wasting the opportunity of higher education to indulge in elaborate accounts of their victimhood instead of studying about the great world at large and preparing to integrate themselves successfully into it.

I came to love Edward. He was twenty-seven years older than I—I was thirty-five, he sixty-two when we met—old enough to be my father, though he never played the role of father in my life. (I already had a fine father of my own and didn't require a second one.) Nor was he my mentor, but then the very thought of being a "mentee" (what a word!) is repellent to me. He was, instead, a friend of wider experience, deeper learning, and grander wit than I. (When I would say something he found amusing, he would often ask, "Did you just make that up?") All that and an inestimable influence.

Edward liked a good joke, not least those featuring national character. One of his favorites asked, What was the difference between a Hungarian and a Romanian? The answer to which is that either will sell you his grandmother, but the Romanian won't deliver. He was not in the least coarse, but amused by coarseness in others.

Saul went in for jokes with a sharp point. A joke of his I have not forgot tells of a young man, Heshele, in the shtetl of Frampol who fears conversation with women. His mother tells him he need not be afraid, for all women like to talk about three things: family, food, and philosophy. One day a young woman named Sasha Goodstein comes to Frampol, and a meeting with the bachelor Heshele is set up for the two of them. She is large, overweight, and expressionless. He finds himself alone in a room with her. Unnerved, he tries to recall his mother's advice about what women like to talk about. Oh, yes, he recalls, family, food, and philosophy. "Sasha," he says, "do you have a brother?" "No," she returns in a gruff voice. "I have no brother." "Sasha," he asks, "do you like noodles?" "No," she says, "I don't like noodles." Family, food, oh, yes, he remembers, philosophy. "Sasha," he asks, "if you had a brother, would he like noodles?" The point of the joke, for those who have lived outside of contemporary universities, is that current-day philosophy often seems to come down to nothing more significant than if you had a brother would he like noodles.

Saul's conversation was lively, sharp, gossipy. I once remarked to him that I thought Joe DiMaggio impressive in taking care of all the details of Marilyn Monroe's funeral after her death by suicide. He informed me that Arthur Miller, who was married to Monroe after DiMaggio, told him, Saul, that DiMaggio beat her up fairly often. "The other side of brutality," Saul said, "is often sentimentality." I once characterized the behavior of an intellectual acquaintance of ours as insecure. "Insecure?" Saul said. "Whatever happened to a good old-fashioned word like 'cowardly'?"

A few paragraphs back I referred to Edward Shils as an "inestimable influence." Except perhaps in early youth, one doesn't look about for influences. At thirty-five, when I first met Edward, neither did I. Nor do I believe he made any earnest attempt to influence me. Such influence as passed down from him to me came from my being so much in his company, which is to say that it came quite by the way. Being around Edward was above all amusing, well worth the forty-or-so-mile drive up and back between our apartments. In his company I laughed a lot.

One morning he called to report that the night before he dreamed he was made a cardinal. "I was allowed to wear the clothes, and looked especially good in the hat," he said. "I walked freely among the Vatican treasures and was allowed to rummage round in the secret archives. Lesser clergy paid obeisance to me. And the best thing of all was that I didn't have to believe any of that bullshit." Here I should add that, despite this comment, Edward was generally respectful of religion, and called himself "a pious agnostic," by which he meant that toward religion generally he felt genuine piety, even

though religious faith wasn't available to him.

Over the years Edward had internationalized himself. The son of a Philadelphia cigar maker, while studying at the London School of Economics after the war he had acquired a mid-Atlantic accent, so that many people who met him were unsure whether he was an American or an Englishman. His vocabulary was studded with old-fashioned words and phrases. He said "wireless" instead of radio, "district" instead of neighborhood. This was salted with occasional Yiddishisms, some of his own devising: a mess was always a *hegdish*, trivial work was *kakapitze*. He kept up a formidable formality, continuing to call many people he had known for decades as well as students he much liked by Mr. or Miss or Mrs. I always felt a touch privileged that he soon called me by my first name and allowed me to call him by his: we were from the first, Joseph (never Joe) and Edward (never Ed).

Edward never learned to drive a car nor to type. He kept a small television set hidden away in one of his guest rooms, but the only time

I ever heard him mention it was when he allowed he had watched the Ronald Reagan–Jimmy Carter presidential debates. Students drove him round the city to pick up his favorite foods or to dine out. Soon I took up the role of chauffeur, which I didn't in the least mind, for his dazzling conversation well repaid the inconvenience. I was pleased to be able to introduce Edward to Ben Moy's extraordinary Chinese restaurant, the Bird, which he came to love, and Mr. Moy soon gave him the run of the place, including the kitchen.

Apart from the three or so months he spent in England, where he was a fellow at Peterhouse College, Cambridge, I don't believe a week ever passed in the nearly twenty-five years I knew him when we didn't get together at least once. When in this country, he called me almost daily, always with a bit of information, a touch of gossip, a joke to tell. I had come to think of him as my dearest friend. I'm not sure that he felt the same about me, but I should be immensely pleased if it were so.

Conversation with Edward was inexhaustibly interesting, often taking surprising turns. "You and I have talked about a great many literary subjects, Joseph," he once said to me, "but we are both too sophisticated ever to talk about Shakespeare." (By which he meant, of course, what could one possibly say.) "Take me home, Joseph," he said to me another time, "where I can make up some new stories

about society." (By which he meant that social science was unlikely ever to grasp the true complexity of human society.) He was amusingly accurate on intellectuals and the professoriat. Of Maurice Cowling, a Cambridge don, he told me: "He's very good for loading the pistols for others to shoot." (By which he meant that Cowling was a trouble-maker without real courage.)

Edward had brought Saul Bellow onto the Committee on Social Thought at the University of Chicago. But over the years their relationship had soured. In one of his early letters, Saul wrote, "I love Edward Shils." Years later, he wrote, "Edward Shils is a boil." I don't know all that had gone on between them to destroy their friendship, but by the time I came to know both men, it was well on its way to ruination. Edward rarely referred to Saul other than with an edge of irony.

On occasion I would get back-to-back telephone calls from Saul and Edward, each putting the other down.

"Joe, Saul here. What's doing?"

"Nothing much. I had dinner last night at Edward's."

"Oh. Does he still have a leather palate?"

The put-down here was that Edward fancied himself a gourmand, someone who enjoys delicacies and lots of them.

"Joseph, Edward."

"I just got off the phone with Saul."

"Ah, our Saul. Saul is the kind of Jew who sits on a backward-turned kitchen chair, pushes his hat back, and tells you he wants to talk turkey."

Edward began to refer to Saul, at least to me, as "the old gentleman," for Saul did not age well. Edward, meanwhile, had the gift of perpetual middle-age; in the twenty-odd years I knew him he seemed not to age at all.

What I believe was behind much of this mutual animosity was Edward's criticism of Saul's behavior, especially with women. He mocked his flirtatiousness. (Saul was a relentless flirt.) He felt he kept poor female company. When Saul was chairman of the Committee on Social Thought, Edward opposed his giving teaching jobs to former lady friends. "I'm not about to let Saul use the committee as a retirement home for his old *navkas*," he once told me. On another occasion, reviewing the manuscript of James Atlas's biography of Saul, which Atlas had asked him to do, Edward said, "Mr. Atlas will never get our friend Saul right until he realizes that if Saul were allowed to spend two hours on the lap of the Queen of England, he would emerge with two observations: 1. she doesn't understand the condition of the modern artist, and 2. she's an anti-Semite." The point here, trenchant as all Edward's humorous remarks were, is that these two items came near to exhausting Saul's interests as a novelist.

I somehow was able to maintain a friendship with both men until, one day, I appeared on a panel in New York sponsored by an organization called the Committee for the Free World, where I remarked that Saul had said—wisely, I thought—that American writers had not, as so many European writers had, directly faced the devils of fascism and communism and thus in their works they fell back on comedy and irony. A woman in the audience named Phyllis Miller had evidently reported back to Saul in some distorted form what I had said, implying it was a criticism of him. Saul never called me about it, but instead dropped off of the Committee for the Free World, on which he had been a member, and made it plain, in his letter of resignation, that I had somehow insulted him. In fact, no insult was intended, nor any given. He had not only made the remark to me but had also made it in one of his many interviews. I later wrote a story based on a Saul-like character who gave many interviews with the title "Another Rare Visit with Noah Danzig."

Saul's break with me may also have had something to do with

my deepening friendship with Edward. How to describe this friendship? He widened my world by introducing me to various intellectual figures of international reputation. Being around Edward was like being in the company of a great stand-up comic. Of the sociologist Robert Merton, a Jew who tried to pass himself off as Gentile, Edward remarked, "At least Robert never took unfair advantage of being Jewish." Edward taught one quarter at Reed College, and twenty minutes into his first class a student raised his hand to tell Edward that at Reed the professor does not lecture, but is a facilitator. "See here," Edward replied, "I did not come two thousand miles to listen to the talk of children. I shall now continue my lecture." His conversation was larded—perhaps I should say chicken-fatted—with Yiddish. The word *tines*, meaning "grievance," as in "he has *tines*" against me, came up with some regularity.

When Edward was discovered to have cancer and people asked him how he was, he would answer, "Apart from dying, not at all bad." Around this time, he asked me to buy him a jar of Shav, a green borscht-like Jewish soup, which he remembered from his childhood. He tasted it, and said: "One of the pleasures of dying is that I shall never again have to eat this soup." After two unsuccessful bouts of chemotherapy, it became clear that Edward had run out of time, and he repaired to his deathbed. At one point Saul called to ask if he could come over to visit him. Edward told Thomas Donovan, an old friend who now served as his caregiver, to tell Saul no, he'd rather he not come over. "I don't want to make it easy for the son of a bitch," he told me.

Saul frequently used his novels to even scores—he was the Blue Beard of novelists when it came to his four ex-wives—and now did so with the deceased Edward. In *Ravelstein,* his last novel, he created a minor character clearly based on Edward, whom he describes as possessing a pretentious library, who has a musty smell, and who is probably homosexual. None of these things was true of Edward, but let that pass. When I read the novel, I thought myself lucky that Saul had died before he had got round to putting me in one of his novels, perhaps as a hustler, a hack writer, an intellectual social climber.

Literary influence is famously difficult to account for with any precision, but my friendship with Edward Shils changed the way I thought and thereby wrote. After spending so much time with him, the world seemed a richer and more interesting, a more various and amusing place. Writing about that world, correspondingly, became both more challenging and exciting. I generally wrote easily, but now I felt even more eager to write, and seemed fairly easily to turn out a great many essays, reviews, short stories. I couldn't wait, you might say, to see what I had to say. I owed this new enthusiasm, as I owed my newly enlarged view of the world, its comedy and its seriousness both, to my dear friend Edward. I miss him still.

The only poem I have ever published has the title "Edward Shils in Heaven," and runs:

Dear Edward, sleepless, lonely, I think of you tonight
In Heaven, out for a leisurely stroll, yet ready for a fight.
Before illogic, false sentiment, sophistry you could never bend,
Now five years dead, why change, allow mere Heaven to forfend?
Master of blistering tirade, scorching academic cant,

Skewering intellectual charade with terrifying rant.
You were the best of haters and for the best of reasons,
Blasting all the virtuous clerks and all their little treasons.
A lover of courage, Dickens, Dunhill's ink in deepest green,
Useful shops, dark thick soups, competence, spiced up aubergine.
Has Heaven food fiery and rich enough for your ample need?
Are there good books and journals in the place for you to read?
Have you discovered an angel with your gift for repartee?
Did you abandon salty Yiddish, shift to Quaker thou and thee?
Pious agnostic, I cannot picture you sitting at God's knee.
Sweet curmudgeon, do you ever think of me?

Chapter Seventeen

Stet, Delete & To Kum

After the death of Edward Shils in 1995 and my departure from the *American Scholar* in 1997, I traveled less, saw fewer people. My wife's and my social life, never widespread to begin with, became even more circumscribed. We went out less and less, invited fewer and fewer people to our home. My own writing became even more the center of my days.

Before leaving New York, I had begun to write book reviews for the *New Republic.* I continued to do so once back in Little Rock. The literary editor of the *New Republic* in those days was Bob Evett, who was also a composer and the magazine's music critic. He was most generous to me, allowing me to write about Max Beerbohm's poems, Tom Wolfe's early journalism, and much else that took my fancy. One review I sent to him was returned to me with radical cuts and botched transitions. When I called Bob to complain, he said, "Oh, that's just Gilbert [Harrison, then the owner and editor in chief of the *New Republic*]. Since his wife died, he gets drunk at lunch, then comes back to the office to edit copy. Just tell me you want everything restored as you wrote it, and I'll do so." This was my first inkling that editors could be troublesome.

A few years later, when I published my article on urban renewal in *Harper's*, Marion Sanders, the editor of the article, sent the edited version back to me with several swatches of it rewritten by her. Her rewrites were not terrible, but they were not my writing. I was thereby presented with the question of whether or not to accept them. With authorial pride—vanity might be more accurate—I decided not to do so, taking the risk that the article may have been turned back to me unpublished. Pleasing to report, it wasn't.

The one review I published in the *New York Review of Books*, a biography of William Benton, the advertising man who was the owner and publisher of the *Encylopaedia Britannica*, was returned to me by Robert Silvers, the editor, with a number of queries about who sat on various Britannica, Inc. boards and others that were in search of capitalist conspiracies. What must have been my unsatisfactory answers did not turn Silvers against running the review. Yet I was never again invited to write for the *New York Review*, chiefly, I suspect, for my having noted, in print, that its contributors were—thank you, Noël Coward—mainly mad dogs and Englishmen.

I had two slight comic pieces—in those days, casuals they were called—in the *New Yorker*, then under the editorship of William Shawn, one of the great editors of the day and whom I never met. I dealt instead with Roger Angell, who wrote on baseball and much else for the magazine. I later wrote eight or nine pieces for the *New Yorker* when it was edited by Tina Brown. What is noteworthy here is that, not long before this, in the *Times Literary Supplement*, I likened Tina Brown's taking over the editorship of the *New Yorker* to finding out that a once elegant friend who, finding a novelty store on the way home from work, began dropping rubber feces and vomit on his friends' rugs. She, Ms. Brown, could not have missed reading this, yet encouraged my contributions to the magazine nevertheless. When Tina Brown departed the *New Yorker* and David Remnick replaced her as editor, he wrote me a pleasing note to the effect that he would be interested in running anything I cared to write for the magazine. Alas, it never happened. I write "alas" chiefly because, though the *New Yorker* is nowhere near the magazine it once was, when William Shawn gave it a liberal spirit without descending to party politics, in its day it had the best of audiences. When I wrote for it, I received responses to my pieces from physicians who in later life had studied ancient Greek, housewives in Texas, who had a thorough yet not in the least pedantic command of grammar, and other unpredictable yet pleasing readers.

Writers, it has been said (I may have been the one who said it), write not for general readers but for editors. An editor I loved writing for was Fred Morgan of the *Hudson Review*, who toward the end of his life ran essays, reviews, and stories of mine. He had a taste for the intellectually deflationary, and among his regular contributors were a killer critic named Marvin Mudrick and the highbrow film one named Vernon Young. I wrote put-downs for Fred of the advent of French theory in American English departments and of the poets Robert Lowell ("Mistah Lowell—He Dead") and Elizabeth Bishop ("Never a Bridesmaid"), which he welcomed with his pleasing enthusiasm.

At the *Times Literary Supplement*, I wrote for John Gross, who soon became a valued friend. The *TLS* enjoyed some of its liveliest days under John, who, in a revolutionary act, put an end to the paper's tradition of anonymous reviewing, a practice that hid many editorial sins: reviewers attacking rivals behind the veil of anonymity, others secretly dominating entire fields, still others bringing their politics to bear without openly owning up to them. John allowed me to write at length on congenial subjects. The fees the *TLS* paid were less than grand, but I felt my own writing in the best of good company, for almost all of John's reviewers seemed superior writers or scholars, and this was fee enough.

I was always pleased to receive John's telephone calls, either from London or New York, when he worked for a while on the *New York Times.* He generally had delicious gossip to report—"Joe, guess with whom Fidel Castro is sleeping?"—or amusing stories to recount. In one of his reviews at the *New York Times* he described Georgi Plekhanov as "the father of Russian Marxism," which caused an ignorant copyeditor on the paper to call it into question. After arguing with this copyeditor for a bit, John suggested a compromise: "All right, then, let's call him 'the uncle of Russian Marxism'?" I put John on the editorial board of the *American Scholar*, where his presence seemed to light up the room. John's successor at the *TLS*, Ferdinand Mount, called upon me to write reviews, among them the official history of the *TLS* itself. After Mount departed, I was never again asked to write for the paper.

I wrote an essay for *Encounter*, then under the editorship of Melvin Lasky, with the title "A Farewell to Utopia" that was the featured piece in the journal's April 1988 issue. I also wrote for Mel an attack on the memoirs of William Phillips, then the coeditor of *Partisan*

Review, under the title "Polonius Remembers." Mel was known for his logorrhea and for his socialist cliches—"hoist by his own petard," "a pleasure to cross swords with my old ideological rival"—but he kept them out of my writing. When he died, in 2004, *Encounter* died with him.

The biographical note currently affixed to my writing for *Commentary* reads: "Joseph Epstein has written for *Commentary* for sixty years." The minutes, hours, days, months, years pass at roughly the same speed, and it is only the decades that seem to fly by. I first published in *Commentary* in 1963, a review of a book by Robert Penn Warren called *Who Speaks for the Negro?* I've since published under three different *Commentary* editors—Norman Podhoretz, Neal Kozodoy, John Podhoretz—more than two hundred further reviews, essays, short stories. No other magazine has been so hospitable to my writing, whether on the subjects of academic freedom, Matthew Arnold, grief, taste, Anton Chekhov, polymaths, pussycats, Montaigne, or Roman history.

For a period in the early 1980s, I was *Commentary*'s critic of contemporary fiction. Each month I turned in roughly five-thousand-word critiques of the novels and stories of Robert Stone, John Irving, John Updike, Ann Beattie, Norman Mailer, Philip Roth, Gabriel García Márquez, Cynthia Ozick, Renata Adler, and Joan Didion. I also wrote in praise of Marguerite Yourcenar and attempted to resuscitate the literary reputation of James Gould Cozzens. Writing out of a highbrow prospective, I found most of this fiction wanting. I also wrote "Who Killed Poetry?" for *Commentary*, an essay of 1988 that caused a small stir, with two issues of the *Association of Writers and Writing Programs* journal devoted to responding to it. *Commentary*, like baseball to José Jiménez, "has been berry berry good to me."

I also wrote a fair amount for the *Weekly Standard*, during its run from 1995 to 2018. The editors there—William Kristol, Fred Barnes—ran longish (three thousand or so words) book reviews of mine and a number of essays on culture generally. I wrote several casuals, or eight-hundred-or-so-word pieces on the endless oddities of language, profanity, hot dogs, failing to buy the favorite wing chair of George Santayana, my mailman, hardware stores, the acknowledgments in books, and anything else that struck my fancy.

Learning to write at short length became useful when I turned to writing op-ed pieces, at first for the *New York Times*, later and more regularly for the *Wall Street Journal*. Getting decently paid to express one's opinions keeps one from being perpetually ticked off or dragged down by the state of the world and the majority of dopes who seem to be in charge of it. "Credulity and Falsehood copulate," Paul Valéry wrote, "and give birth to Opinion," an amusing aphorism that hasn't stopped me from expressing mine.

In his dealings with Hollywood the best arrangement for a writer is to have his book or story sold for a million dollars, and then the movie, which figures vastly to corrupt his work, never gets made. My own dealings with Hollywood have satisfied only the second of these desiderata: I have made much smaller sums from Hollywood for movies that never got made. The first was a payment, with apologies from the producer for its pathetic (by Hollywood standards) sum of $70,000, to write a script for a story of mine called "The Goldin Boys." I wrote the script, but the producer was not long after fired by Warner Bros. and the movie never got made. Stanley Jaffe, the producer (of *Kramer vs. Kramer*, *Fatal Attraction*, *The Accused*), three times acquired an option (for $10,000 each time) on my story "Don Juan

Zimmerman," but no movie was ever made of it. Finally, a friend named Maury Rosenfield, who with his wife produced the movie *Bang the Drum Slowly*, wanted to make a movie from my story "Moe," but he died before he could do so. No business, I guess, like show business.

I have also won a prize or two: the Harold U. Ribalow and the Edward Lewis Wallant prizes for fiction, the Midland Authors for nonfiction, the *Chicago Tribune* Heartland Prize for a book of my literary criticism, the Harold Washington Literary Award, and a National Medal for the Humanities. Of the last, an acquaintance remarked that it was a shame I had to win it under the presidency of George W. Bush. I responded by remarking that, yes, I should much have preferred to have won it under Abraham Lincoln, but, then, one couldn't have everything. That I won my National Humanities Medal under George W. Bush demonstrates that, in a much divided America, literary and other prizes are, by and large, given out to people on the basis of what are perceived to be their politics. No conservative is likely to win a Pulitzer Prize or a MacArthur Fellowship, no progressive a Bradley Prize. (Edward Shils wrote, in longhand, an eleven-page recommendation for me for a MacArthur Fellowship, but to no avail.) Presidential awards—the Freedom Medal or the ones for the humanities and the arts—are given out to those thought to be either conservatives or progressives according to the politics of the president then in office. The sadness of this, from the point of view of a prize recipient, is the knowledge that one's prize has been diluted by politics and thereby doesn't carry anything like the weight of unanimity it ought to carry.

Occasionally, perhaps once or twice a month, I am recognized on the street by strangers. "Aren't you Joseph Epstein, the writer?"

they ask. "I am," I sometimes reply, "though I see this disguise hasn't worked." This sort of fame, the pleasures of recognition, doesn't much interest me. I much prefer my prose style be recognized than my person.

I have been able to publish more than thirty books. This qualifies me to fall under that most ambiguous of rubrics for writers: prolific. A number of these books have been translated into Chinese, Japanese, Czech, Italian, and other languages. None has brought in enough money to allow me to buy Twitter, but a few have done quite decently financially. My *Snobbery: The American Version* earned, after its paperback sale, roughly half a million dollars. One of my books of short stories, *Fabulous Small Jews*, continues to have a modest sale more than twenty years after its original publication. One day some years ago I received an email from a man named Hunter Lewis, who ran a financial firm that advised a number of Ivy League schools on how to invest their endowments and was the publisher of Axios Press, informing me that he admired my writing and would be pleased to publish anything of mine that had not already been published in book form. Hunter Lewis subsequently brought out five thick and handsome collections of my essays. Two volumes of my correspondence with the novelist and screenwriter Frederic Raphael have also found publishers. Four volumes of my short stories have been published. I am without complaint.

I am not about to prophesy whether any of this abundant scribbling of mine will last much beyond my lifetime. I think here of the essayist and caricaturist Max Beerbohm, another figure in my personal pantheon of literary heroes. In a letter to John Bohun Lynch, who was about to write his biography, Beerbohm wrote: "My gifts are small, I've used them well and discreetly, never straining them, and the result is that I've made a charming little reputation." While still alive, Beerbohm estimated that he had fifteen hundred readers in England and perhaps another thousand in America. Might I claim more, or even as many? I don't know, but I would settle for that number or even fewer if they were, as Max Beerbohm's readers have always been, devoted ones. To wish to be read after one is dead is, hope against hope, the vanity of all vanities. But, then, no one ever claimed that modesty is among the first qualifications for being a writer.

Chapter Eighteen

Big D, Distinctly Not Dallas

I began this book in the summer of 2022. I am ending it now, in the summer of 2023, at the age of eighty-six. Eighty-six is an age where death is no longer a rumor. Family members, friends, acquaintances are regularly taken out of the game, and one thinks more than a bit about when one will oneself depart the planet. One thinks quite as much about whether one's life had any effect, if not on the world at large then at least on one's friends and family. How, one wonders, has one acted one's own part in the comedy of life?

People speak about running out of friends as one grows old. I have myself felt this for some while now, having for fortuitous reasons many good friends eight or more years older than I, among them Hilton Kramer, John Gross, Midge Decter, and Dan Jacobson. As one grows old, there are fewer people to look up to, to admire in the way one naturally does those older than oneself who have achieved more. Then one loses many friends among one's contemporaries. Not long ago I thought I would call Bob Swenson, with whom I won the Chicago high school doubles championship. I last saw Bob roughly seven years ago, when he came into Chicago from Philadelphia, where he worked as an epidemiologist at Temple University. I didn't have his phone number, so I googled him, hoping to find it online, only to discover he had died last year, of pneumonia, at eighty-five. We'll never have that talk; I'll never be able to tell him what a good friend I thought him when we were kids. Late life, which brings so much to be grateful for, also has more than its share of subtractions and can be heavily laden with remorse.

Last year, too, my friend David Zimberoff, after struggling fairly successfully for four or so years with Parkinson's, found the disease taking a radical turn for the worse. Unable, or at least unwilling, to live with it any longer, he took himself off to Switzerland, where he underwent an assisted suicide. His doing so threw me; for weeks afterward I could not get out of my mind the picture of him in a chair, a deadening IV in his arm, listening to music, awaiting in inexorable solitude the arrival of death.

"Let your last thinks all be thanks," wrote W. H. Auden, who himself died in 1973 at the age of sixty-six. I wake every morning, touch the top of the night table beside my bed, and say, "Thank you for another day." Doing so, I often think of the mother-in-law of a friend of mine, who suffered pains from various illnesses and who woke each morning and exclaimed, "Shit!" because she hadn't died in her sleep the night before.

George Santayana remarked that one of the reasons older people often grow grumpy about the world is that, with the presentiment of their own death, they can't see what good the world can be without them in it. He also claimed that whatever one's age, it makes sense to assume one will live ten years longer. He himself died at eighty-eight.

I can easily enough imagine the world without my being in it. Unless one has been an earthshaking character, a Cyrus the Great, a Pericles, an Alexander, a Napoleon, a Churchill, or a villain of the magnitude of Lenin, Stalin, Hitler, or Mao, or a thinker on a level with Plato, Aristotle, Descartes, Spinoza, Kant, Hegel, or Locke, or a writer with the gifts of a Homer, Dante, Shakespeare, Cervantes, Dickens, Proust, Mann, one's presence on earth is not, in the long view, likely to have much mattered. In this cruel long view, my best hope is to be remembered fifty or so years from now by my three grandchildren, and then, *poof!*, it's bye-bye, Mr. American Pie. I hope my grandchildren will remember me as kindly, generous, good-humored. More than this I cannot expect.

I had a neighbor named Dee Crosby, unmarried, a grade school teacher, roughly ten years older than I, an earnest, mass-attending Catholic, who one day told me that death didn't in the least worry her. "I hope to avoid a painful or a sloppy death," she said. "But death itself is not a problem, for I know where I am going." A few years later, while in hospice, Dee called me to report a strong craving for Chinese food. I brought some to her bedside, where I found her awaiting death, yet still cheerful. Watching her tuck into her Chinese food, I felt a stab of faith envy, wishing I could myself be so confident as she of a pleasing afterlife. Is it possible to believe in a higher power and yet not, in the conventional religious sense, have faith that that power is looking after one? It had better be, for this is my condition.

Rosemary Clooney sings that "if you're worried and you can't sleep, just count your blessings instead of sheep." I have quite a few—blessings, that is, not sheep. Allow me to count some of them here.

Never having had extravagant tastes—for those $200 bottles of wine, $600 dinner-for-two bills, first-class air travel, $2,000 suits—I have saved enough over the years not to worry unduly about money. Although I never expected it when I set out in life, I am, owing to my *American Scholar* and Northwestern jobs, a pensioner. My condition here does not much differ from that set out in the lyrics of "September Song": "I have lost one tooth [in my case more than one] and I walk a little lame [on occasion I go out with a cane] . . . But I have a little money and I have a little fame." I hope I still have sufficient time for the waiting game.

Still in the blessing count, my health remains decent. (Pause here while I knock on wood.) I have never jogged, or worked out, or played a sport beyond the age of fifty, when a minor leg injury forced me to quit racquetball. At sixty I underwent bypass heart surgery, which I went into with surprising sangfroid and came out of well. Shouldn't be a total loss, as the punch line of an old Jewish joke has it. I wrote an essay on the subject, "Taking the Bypass," that ran in the *New Yorker.* A few years ago I fell, as older guys are wont to do, and, as I mentioned earlier, fractured my femur, which required surgery and three days in an obstetrics hospital, but left no serious aftereffects. My weight is normal, and I eat whatever I want, including lots of ice cream. I have come to define good health as Bill Bryson does in his book *The Body: A Guide for Occupants*, that one is healthy so long as one hasn't had a physical recently. The Romans were on to this long ago, advising: *Bene caca et declina medicos.*

I seem, in fact, to have become the reverse of a hypochondriac, which is to say that I tend to ignore small physical woes: what must be a touch of arthritis in my left hand, an occasional itchiness in my left ear, not always regular elimination, rather heavy breathing after carrying a shopping bag with groceries for a few blocks, less than perfect sleep. Going down a staircase, any staircase, I search for the banister. Walking about, I keep my eyes on the sidewalk lest I fall again. I do not mention these ailments or precautions to anyone. Were I to do so to my primary care physician, she would likely send me for density tests, stress tests, CAT scans, MRIs, SATs, Lord knows what else. But, then, I seem to have become my own primary care physician.

Not least among my blessings has been my family, which includes a good-hearted, tolerant, and devoted wife, a savvy and thoughtful son—whenever anyone asks my age, I note that I have a son who is retired, which suggests I must myself be beyond forty—and three elegant and interesting grandchildren.

Far from least among my blessings has been my being able to continue writing well into my eighties. (I currently owe book reviews to three different editors.) Writing still gives me great pleasure. I have never been afflicted with writer's block or have made a great drama over literary creation. (Was it the sportswriter Red Smith who said that writing was easy, "All you have to do is sit down at the typewriter, cut open a vein, and bleed"?) I have received more than my share of praise for my various writings, some from critics, some from common readers, some from people I myself have much admired. I have attained an age where attacks on what I write, though I could do just as nicely without them, do not all that much affect me.

What to many people would seem a dull life, mine, I find calmly satisfying. My daily routine consists of writing in the morning, lunching mostly at home, reading in the afternoon, watching sports or movies in the evening. I have lost all interest in travel. If you were to offer me, rent free, an apartment in Paris for the month of July, throwing in enough of your air miles for first-class travel and noting that the refrigerator in the apartment is filled with splendid French food, I should find a way not to take you up on your offer. I like things too much as they are in my own apartment and on my own routine. I prefer to have my library of a thousand or so books at hand, the sights and sounds of my neighborhood outside my door, my surviving friends nearby.

Older people, confronted with the prospect of travel, tend to weigh the pleasures against the pain, and usually find the latter easily outweighs the former. I know I do. Nearly half a century ago I took great pleasure in a Swann's cruise of Greece and the Dalmatian coast; today the thought of any cruise, with its cargo of what Henry James called "my detested fellow pilgrims," sounds a torture. In his diary, apropos of travel, Noël Coward wrote: "People are always telling me about something I just missed. I find it very restful."

As I grow older, I also find my interests narrowing. Whole issues of the *New York Review of Books* often do not contain a single piece I care to read. Years ago, I ceased reading about politics at any length. The apparently highly valued writers for the *New Yorker*—Adam Gopnik, Hilton Als, Louis Menand, Malcolm Gladwell—seem to me good students merely, and nowhere near so compelling as the writers I found in the *New Yorker* when I began reading it in college. I regularly drop and then a few years later pick up my subscription to that once exalted magazine. I recently canceled my subscription to the *London Review of*

Books, whose anti-Israel politics I found noxious. I read a fair amount of the *TLS*, chiefly those reviews about the classics, philosophy, and the (preponderantly dead) writers I admire. I haven't read the *New York Times Book Review* or *Magazine* in more than a decade and don't believe that I've missed much. In my desultory reading I continue to come up with, for me, new discoveries: the autobiography of John Buchan and his splendid biography of Augustus, the essays of Gilbert Highet, the fiction of Milton Steinberg. One of the splendid things about reading is that one is never out of business.

I haven't been to a movie theater in more than a decade, though I used to think myself an inveterate moviegoer. Most movies in recent years, or so I conclude from commercials about them I see on television, are for children or adults who never left childhood. Instead I live off the movies of the past, found on Turner Classic Movies or on Netflix. The same goes for plays. The supposedly great playwrights of the past century—Arthur Miller, Tennessee Williams, Samuel Beckett, Bertolt Brecht, Edward Albee—I find dreary, their plays an intellectual punishment to sit through. If the current century has produced any impressive new playwrights, I do not know of them. I used to go to classical music concerts fairly regularly, but then began to discover that during these concerts my mind wandered and left the room. While Mozart's *Requiem* is being played, I look about and wonder if the man two rows in front of me and three seats to the left isn't wearing a toupee, or why the woman seated next to me needed to use her entire bottle of Chanel No. 5 for this concert. Decent seats for two at a play or concert now cost $400 or more, and those for sporting events are not less. Best to stay home and watch *The Maltese Falcon* for the sixth time.

In his autobiography, *Persons and Places*, Santayana noted that he, too, no longer cared to attend concerts, and preferred to stand listening to street musicians in Italy. I listen to music on CDs at home or in my car. Santayana also wrote: "Never have I enjoyed youth so thoroughly as I have in my old age. . . . I have drunk the pleasures of life more pure, more joyful, than ever it was when mingled with all the hidden anxieties and little annoyances of actual living. Nothing is inherently and invincibly young except spirit. And spirit can enter a human being perhaps better in the quiet of old age and dwell there more undisturbed than in the turmoil of adventure."

This youthful surge one discovers in one's eighties brings with it a sense of detachment. By one's eighties one finds less use for the future tense; one lives more day by day, spending a fair amount of those days thinking about the past. "As one ages," John Buchan wrote in *Memory Hold-the-Door*, his autobiography, "the memory seems to be inverted, and recent events to grow dim in the same proportion as ancient happenings become clear." On local television news the other day I noted a new series of buildings is going up on the South Side of Chicago that will be completed in 2035 and thought I won't be around to see them occupied. If I were to die tomorrow, no one reading my obituary would feel that I have been in the least deprived of a full span of years. When one doesn't expect to be around all that much longer, one would hate to check out while reading, say, a long article in the *New York Times Magazine* with the title "Thailand Fights for Democracy."

Detachment brings its own pleasures. Things would doubtless be different if I were a more political person or otherwise more activist in spirit than I have been throughout my life. I have been reading

Reaching Ninety, a memoir by Martin Duberman, a left-wing activist, who has measured his life chiefly by the progress of the causes he has fought for over his life: gay liberation, anti-racism, the struggle generally for equality here in America, the advent of socialism round the world. Martin Duberman finds Bernie Sanders's socialism inadequate, and his politics are distinctly not mine. But his activism has given his life a shape of sorts and a gauge by which to calibrate its success or failure.

My own role in life has been largely spectatorial. I have spent most of my years on the sidelines, glass of wine in hand, entertained by the mad swirl of the circus put on by humanity, trying to figure out what is and is not important in life. I have, from time to time, put down the glass of wine and, in essays, reviews, short stories, written up my findings. Chief among them is that the world, for all its faults, flaws, faux pas, remains an amusing place.

Life for me in its variety, its richness, its surprises and astonishments has not come near to losing its fascination. I should like to hang around at least as long as my father, who died at ninety-two, and renegotiate my departure then. This would give me plenty of time to work on my deathbed words, for thus far the best I have been able to come up with is "I should have ordered the Mongolian beef."

Acknowledgments

Some while ago I wrote that I did not plan to write an autobiography and chose instead to spend some of the details of my life in nickels and dimes in various of my published essays. Now in the autobiography I have written, a large number of these details reappear in recycled form. The moral of the story, if it has one, is that one must never completely believe a writer, at least about the future of his own work.

I would like to acknowledge the help in the composition of this book of Robert Messenger, former student, longtime friend, and brilliant editor.

Index

About the Author

JOSEPH EPSTEIN is the author of thirty-one books, among them works on divorce, ambition, snobbery, friendship, envy, and gossip. He has published seventeen collections of essays and four books of short stories. He has been the editor of the *American Scholar*, the intellectual quarterly of Phi Beta Kappa, and for thirty years he taught in the English department at Northwestern University. He has written for the *New Yorker*, *Commentary*, the *New Criterion*, the *Times Literary Supplement*, *Claremont Review of Books*, the *New York Review of Books*, *Poetry*, and other magazines both in the United States and abroad. In 2003, he was awarded the National Humanities Medal.